SHOW UP HARD

SHOW
UP

A ROAD MAP FOR
HELPERS IN CRISIS

HARD

SHANNON WEBER, MSW

Author photo: Vincent Carrella/The Light House Photography
Book cover and interior design: Sheba Sanders
Street map art created by Freepik
Production: Margit Pschick

ISBN-13 #9781730821134

PRAISE FOR SHANNON WEBER'S *SHOW UP HARD*

Shannon Weber changes lives.

In a world of change and challenging workplaces, her workshops teach the "soft skills" that make great leaders truly great. I've personally seen the transformation of hundreds of people who have worked with Shannon and used her teachings to raise the bar in their work.

If you are looking to improve company culture, connect with employees, and truly make a difference, this is the place.

Fraser Larock
Business Development, Seth Godin's altMBA

Shannon Weber is so much more than the sum of her remarkable contributions. Her openhearted approach to every single day, her relentless intellect bound tight with her incisive disdain for the pretentious, and her truly kaleidoscopic energy swirl together to create this marvelous person I feel so honored to know. Her greatest contribution to us all is her gift for living.

Jay MacGillvary
Registered Midwife and Co-Director, Toronto's Positive Pregnancy Program

Shannon Weber is courageously showing the way to a world where love and generosity can sit within clear boundaries, and where compassion can thrive. I am grateful for the hope this gives all of us in human services.

Helen Sanderson
Founder, Wellbeing Teams

The reality of the modern world and workplace is that humans bring their entire selves to work.

Life's unexpected twists and turns never miss an address. Dealing with difficult conversations and circumstances can make or break the best projects or intentions. And the best leaders know that having the tools to navigate and support their teams through tough situations is one of the powerful ways that they can be of service to those that they lead and the work they do.

Shannon's incredible framework from this book has become a fundamental pillar in the way we approach our work at Seth Godin's altMBA. She transformed the way that we've been able to engage with people, build relationships, scale our company, and troubleshoot even the most challenging problems.

Her approach is simple, yet brilliant—a life skill, one that belongs in the tool kit of any leader looking to make a difference in the lives of others.

Kelli Wood
Provost, Seth Godin's altMBA

What I love about this way of connecting with another human is that it allows for the possibility that people aren't broken or damaged, and that they don't need to be fixed. Showing Up Hard is about being truly present for another human, free of assumptions and judgments, as the softest, truest me I can be.

Rebecca Channer
Founder, ProsperCity

Shannon Weber is a revolutionary. A woman of heart and mind. The collision of her intellect and ocean-deep soul plays out in her day-to-day life, where she understands that constraints and challenges are blessed opportunities for lasting and meaningful change. The Show Up Hard framework is sure to incite readers to redraw their boundaries with lines of empathy and self-awareness. The time is ripe for her work to be made known to leaders in the helping professions, and I anticipate the release of this book to set off a chain reaction of doing good and leveling up.

Jennifer Slepin, MSN RN PHN
Chief Nursing Officer and Founder of HepCarestream: The Nurse Is In

Shannon's training hit me like a bolt of lightning. She helped me see how creating safe spaces for others, and clear boundaries, didn't diminish my caring or generosity. Instead, it allowed it to bloom and flourish. It was a huge revelation.

Mark Dyck
Chief Community Advocate, The Right Company

All my life I've been a pleaser. I've bent myself backwards to help other people, and more times than not, it has backfired. At best, I've been seen and used as a doormat, not as a helpful and valuable resource. At worst, I've ended up tangled in a situation where I offered a helping hand, and the person who needed help took my hand, and then the other, and somehow I got all roped in because I didn't know how to say "no" or "enough." I would get very upset at myself for what I thought was being weak.

The concept of the Compassionate Witness made an enormous impression on me. It gave me the a-ha moment I needed to realize that there is indeed a point where everyone can be well. It has nothing to do with being strong or weak; it is a skill to be developed via this wonderful system Shannon created from her experience. Anyone can apply the framework and—just like a muscle—it becomes better with practice. So I can definitely help, yet I can also ensure my well-being. By being a Compassionate Witness, I don't have to derail my life or put it on hold while going out of my way to help as I did in the past. Instead, I can offer the best of me for the particular situation, while also keeping the best of me to ensure I am well and my life can continue its normal course. It's empowering, enlightening, and enjoyable. Thank you, Shannon!

Helena Escalante
Founder, Speaker, Bibliophile, and Writer at EntreGurus.com

Shannon's Show Up Hard framework has transformed how I interact with my family, friends, and co-workers on a daily basis. Her concepts help me navigate complex human interactions and intentionally design how I show up as a Compassionate Witness. She's taught me the value of setting necessary boundaries so that I can fully support others in a sustainable way. Because of Shannon's work, I'm more effective, resilient, and openhearted as a leader and, more importantly, as a human being.

Ian Scott
Director of Product Strategy, Start With Why

With her simple prompts and warm invitation to share, Shannon has an uncanny ability to not only draw out candid, intimate responses but also give them an audience.

Caroline Kangas
Store Manager, 826 Valencia

Shannon Weber's work in empathy and crisis has helped me learn to lead with greater resiliency. With this, I've been able to build relationships with clearer intent and healthier boundaries. I'm able to show up and make a bigger difference for friends, family, and colleagues.

Marie Schacht
Head Coach, Seth Godin's altMBA

Shannon's training has fundamentally changed the way I think about and navigate my work. Her insights into empathy and navigating conflict shape the way I show up for my clients on a daily basis.

Peter Shepherd
Founder and Coach, Periscope Coaching

Shannon's training gave me a framework to reconsider how I was helping. I had the showing up part down, but I needed some "containers" to help me view and better understand my capacity to help. Shortly after the training I had a chance to give her ideas a practical test drive, and it felt so good to see how much easier it was to make a big difference: reconsidering how I show up.

Adam Lemmon
Founder and Owner, Badass Backpacks

For me, the empathy circles have been such a beautifully simple tool for me to show up in a more useful way for my team, my peers, and my friends. It showed me that while I thought I was being the most supportive person I could be, I was actually doing those who sought my help a disservice. I was more enmeshed than you could possibly be! I now have Shannon's empathy circles drawn for myself on a sticky note on my monitor at work. A little reminder to myself to take a minute and think about how I can be the best Compassionate Witness I can be for people, to ask the right questions, to walk alongside rather than ahead, to help them find the strength in themselves.

Sarah Sprague
Product Leader and Chief of Staff, Envested

Remember that scene from *The Matrix* where Neo puts his hand up, stops the bullets in midair, and then picks one out of the air to examine it? That's what I feel capable of doing now after learning Shannon's circles framework. When life starts to feel like that scene from The Matrix, I'm now able to see it, stop, and examine the "bullets" and myself.

Covington Doan
"Marketing Guy," Stupid Good Coffee

When you help people in critical moments of their lives, it is easy to lose yourself along the way. The concepts helped me to become more conscious in how I show up for others and provide more empathy along the way. It is a practice that takes effort but adds value every time it's considered.

Dirk Lehmann
Startup Advisor and Pitch Coach, Dirk Lehmann & Partners

to
Mom & Dad

Thankyou for
teaching me how
to love and
to be loved.

CONTENTS

INTRODUCTION   **15**

WHAT TO BRING. WHAT TO LEAVE.   **18**

BOOK ONE | EMBARKING   **21**

1 | A Framework For Showing Up   23

2 | Put Yourself On The To-Do List   47

3 | Leading Is A Posture   53

4 | Empathy Is An Adventure   59

5 | Skills To Build For The Journey   75

6 | Embark Before You Are Ready   91

BOOK TWO | DETOURS   **97**

1 | Confusing Leading With Saving   99

2 | Are Your Narratives Your Identity?   105

3 | Empathy Is Not Sympathy   115

4 | Tunnels   123

5 | Leaky Containers   135

6 | Vicarious Trauma   157

BOOK THREE | ARRIVING   **165**

1 | The Intersection Of Empathy And Resilience   167

2 | Automate Resiliency   171

3 | Commit To Possibility   179

4 | Practice Is A Practice   189

5 | Returning To Equilibrium, Changed   195

APPENDIX | PAYING IT FORWARD   **200**

RESOURCES AND SUGGESTED READING   **202**

ACKNOWLEDGMENTS   **208**

ABOUT THE AUTHOR   **210**

INTRODUCTION

Here you are. You are working late into the evening. You've logged back on from your personal computer to complete the grant report that is due tomorrow morning, after you finished the dinner dishes and settled the house for the night. You've been in a continuous text conversation with a co-worker who rushed into your office this afternoon with a family emergency. After your co-worker left work early to attend to her family's needs, you took over her client visits for the rest of the day, managing the disappointment from a change in plans, explaining why there are no more vouchers for the month, and trying to connect high-need individuals with scant services.

After doing the right thing for others, you are now behind on paperwork. You start to fret about tomorrow's site visit because you are not as prepared as you would like to be but also because there are rumored budget cuts. You try to balance these realities with the requests for raises from several key staff members.

This is not how you imagined life would be—giving so much and feeling constantly behind. At times, you feel lost in the swirling overwhelm, looking for direction to steady the pace. You are worthy of much more. You deserve to receive as much as you give every day. Burnout is looming around the corner in the direction you're going.

So let's find a different path, together.

WHO YOU ARE

You are a committed soul in relentless pursuit of creating a better world. Challenging times crave leadership, often on a moment's notice. You manage a team of well-intentioned staff. And you manage up more than you'd like to admit—coaching your supervisors through personal and work crises. Your helper roles are both formal and informal. As a helper you grapple with the immense work to be done while sustaining yourself in the process. You juggle competing priorities, have many requests to consider, and in the process worry you are not doing enough. You Show Up Hard.

Empathetic helpers are those who show up to support possibility in times of tumult and uncertainty. While caring may come easily to you, embodying empathy—the ability to see the world through another's eyes—takes skill, requires maintenance, and demands an ongoing plan for sustenance. Sustaining ourselves for the long haul, learning how to get unstuck, and contributing to a sense of belongingness at work so our colleagues are also buoyed up for the journey is key to success in creating change. Preparing for heart-sinking and heart-racing moments—the events we fear might happen or what keeps us up at night—is the work of a wise leader. Without this preparation and a plan for staying the course, we are fated to burn out as a result. We must learn to sustain ourselves in the crisis so we are not lost, and can show up again.

HOW TO USE THIS BOOK

I love a road trip—the expansiveness of a new view, reading roadside signs, imagining life in towns as they whiz by, encountering unexpected adventures, and stopping and starting when and where we want. While I've transitioned to phone-based map apps to ultimately guide my family's trips, we still purchase printed maps before each journey. Unfolding these maps on the dining-room table adds to the anticipation of the trip. Road maps help us to get started, to be brave, to begin an adventure. In that same way, this book-as-road-map is meant to be a portal for you, to give you ease as you show up for others in challenging times. You can add this Show Up Hard road map to your back pocket or computer bag or even tuck it behind your heart. Keep it with you as you adventure about in the world expanding your capacity for leading with empathy, even as you examine how you choose to show up for others.

Like any good road trip, there are lots of places where we will stop to reflect, to capture a memory or two, or to imagine what we want to happen next. Ultimately, we'll find ourselves at the intersection of empathy and resilience. Keep a pen or pencil handy to write in the margins of the book and complete the prompts in the Reflection Rest Stops. You can also open a voice-recording app on your phone or take notes in your journal. Take whatever time feels necessary to you for the prompts. Completing the prompts is not required to move forward with the book content, but they are excellent conduits to a deeper understanding of the practices. Writing about our internal and external worlds allows us to integrate experiences, move forward, change patterns, and glean insights. Feel free to stop and start, return to certain chapters that resonate, or zip through content you are already familiar with.

I have a habit of writing myself reminders. I write snippets on sticky notes, backs of envelopes, and index cards and even have a temporary-tattoo pen for the very important notes I need to scrawl on my body. I've included Notes to Self throughout the book, wise words that help me stay the course.

However you approach it, make this road trip yours. I am grateful to be on this adventure with you.

Ready? Let's go!

WHAT TO BRING.
WHAT TO LEAVE.

Below is a suggested packing list as we head out on this adventure.
Pack light. Only the essentials are needed.

WHAT TO BRING:
- ✓ Your essence—the core part of who you are when operating as your best self.
- ✓ Your presence.
- ✓ A practice of staying centered.
- ✓ Mad listening skills.
- ✓ Boundaries.
- ✓ Truth telling.

WHAT TO LEAVE:
- ✓ Self-doubt.
- ✓ Your triggers.
- ✓ Accumulated stress and stories from your day or week.
- ✓ Old stories that no longer serve you.
- ✓ Your ego.
- ✓ The past.

NOTE TO SELF

you have what you need.

BOOK ONE

Embarking

One of the greatest gifts we can give another human being is to act as their guardian, to hold space for them.

—Madisyn Taylor

We love our work. We get out of bed for a cause. We are deeply connected and driven. Yet, we've learned the hard way—passion is not a protector from burnout. Proactively planning how we choose to show up for others is the antidote to balancing our commitment to creating change with the finite resources of our emotional labor.

1 | A FRAMEWORK FOR SHOWING UP

"We teach what we most need to learn—we give what we most need to receive."

—Gabor Maté

"Crisis Hotline. This is Shannon. How can I help?" In the late 1990s, I coordinated the Crisis Hotline of Houston. Houston is the fourth largest city in the United States, and Crisis Hotline was the go-to resource for individuals at risk of suicide, in addition to generally connecting callers in need with resources throughout the city. The hotline was staffed 24/7 by volunteers who completed 50 hours of training before beginning shifts answering the telephones. Trained staff and a clinical team backed up the volunteers round the clock. My role was to oversee operations of the hotline, maintaining a high level of customer service for the 65,000 calls received each year while ensuring the volunteers had the tools they needed to succeed and felt supported.

The best people in the world showed up to volunteer. Imagine the commitment! Completing the 50-hour training was just the beginning. Volunteers agreed to work a weekly four-hour shift for a year, including requirements for overnight and weekend shifts. There were volunteers who had worked weekly shifts for multiple years.

Many volunteers had incredible stories from their own lives that led them to want to give back. During part of the training we talked about our own stories—why we chose to show up. A former hotline caller turned volunteer desired to give back. A man who lost his partner of 35 years in a freak accident committed to working the 4 to 8 a.m. shift one morning each week. Young people explored careers in the helping professions. Many had a family member who suffered from any number of crises they felt unable to fully support, and they wanted to realize a more immediate satisfaction of helping. Retirees wanted to keep skills sharp and contribute to the community. Understanding these stories, our motivations, is illuminating. Knowing our connection to why we show up helps us to understand how we show up. The why and the how behind our choice to show up point us toward sustainable solutions for maintaining ourselves in the face of overwhelm and exhaustion.

In the Crisis Hotline model, telephone calls were finished within fifteen minutes, unless there was an active suicide in process and police were involved. It might seem counterintuitive, but with skill and practice you can create a feeling of safety and help someone develop a next-step plan to alleviate a problem in fifteen minutes. There are diminishing returns for creating actionable change after fifteen minutes. In a crisis intervention model, the scope of change you seek to make is the smallest move that will bridge the caller to a place of stability or equilibrium. Let's give this concept context in another setting: Imagine how the course of a hike can radically change if where you begin walking from is shifted by only a few degrees. A few-degree shift in your starting point can land you in a completely different final location. Accepting that radical change begins with one small step in the right direction, a small step chosen by the caller themself, is key to both being an awesome Crisis Hotline volunteer as well as finding meaning in the work.

Crisis Hotline volunteers were trained to: Develop rapport with callers, assess the current situation that had created the crisis or disequilibrium, listen to discover what would help, and make a plan with a caller to support change, including referrals to community organizations and programs.

Crisis Hotline had clear rules and boundaries all volunteers needed to abide by to protect themselves and our callers: Do not share personal details or information. Don't reveal the address of the overnight location. Don't meet callers. Don't bring visitors into the call center. One night near the end of weeks of volunteer training, several new volunteers struggled with the absolute of the rules. It appeared this group of giant-hearted givers did not know—metaphorically—where they ended and the caller began. I get it. There is an inherent desire to do more, coupled with the sometimes counterintuitive truth that less is in fact more powerful.

Social work school had given me the theory and supervised field work had given me the practice to hone those boundaries, which are the basis to begin understanding the balance of giving and receiving. Sometimes we might not know how or where to stop or pause once generous giving starts. Or when the giving loses productivity and becomes enabling. And sometimes we don't know how to begin giving, because the thought is so overwhelming.

As the volunteers questioned some of the hard-and-fast Crisis Hotline guidelines, I decided I would try to visually illustrate this delicate balance. I grabbed a blank overhead-projector transparency (these were once a precious commodity in the nonprofit world!) and drew a series of circles to illustrate different examples of how we might choose to embody our practices of showing up. My goal with these simple illustrations: help volunteers to literally and figuratively see how they could best help others. This circles framework provided a shared understanding for our ongoing conversations about boundaries and supported volunteers in seeing the value of limits. With limits comes the ability to fully lean into the present moment—the now of supporting change. Most importantly, the circles illustrate the power of choosing how we show up depending on the context and situation. This structure enables possibility.

The circles model that originated in my effort to support Crisis Hotline volunteers has come to be a lifeline for myself and heaps of helpers in a variety of settings. In the two-plus decades since, I've shared this framework with thousands of people from a variety of backgrounds. I've been amazed to see the nearly universal relief that comes from learning about and applying the circles framework. I've received hundreds of emails with stories about how people were able to immediately put the framework into practice—Showing Up Hard and feeling steady on the journey.

If crisis hotlines can help people via a telephone call in short, focused windows of time, how might you create an environment where you support others in being their best selves in one-on-one and team meetings? How might this way of engaging contribute to feelings of belongingness at work? How might this framework support you as an empathetic steward of others? How might we drop our guard to be available to others, to encourage vulnerability and connection? We can use the circles framework to create emotional safety in the work setting and to allow for greater vulnerability among those we have stewardship over.

INTRODUCING THE MISSED CONNECTION STYLE OF ENGAGING

"We systematically overestimate the value of access to information and underestimate the value of access to each other."

—Clay Shirky

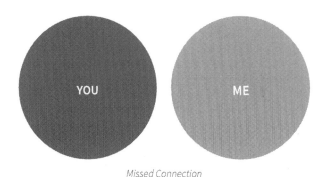

Missed Connection

The name of the Missed Connection framework comes from the proximity of engagement—we are quite literally missing human connection, that is, the possibility for empathy. There is a distance between the two people large enough that likely neither one of them feels satisfied by the interaction, no real change is made.

There is nothing wrong with a Missed Connection, if that is the way of engaging we choose. We have Missed Connection-style interactions all day long as we travel throughout our daily life—on the bus, in the grocery store, at the post office. In these interactions there is no need or compelling why for engaging in a different way.

However, when someone asks us for help or when our work responsibilities include stewardship over other people, a Missed

Connection response may, quite literally, miss the mark. A Missed Connection can happen because of a low emotional intelligence (EQ) response, an "I'm not paying attention" response, a response based on our internal biases or assumptions, or a response that comes from our fear of what might happen if we engage with this particular person or situation.

Missed Connections can be disappointing and cause a disconnect in an existing relationship. As one friend with a terminally ill partner and young children said, "I think it is weird when people at work know what is happening in my life but don't ask me how I am doing."

Another friend shared about his choice to not immediately support a female colleague as she came forward with her #MeToo story: "I did not think it was my place to do something. I did not know what to do. But I've not stopped thinking about it ever since she told me. I know doing something is the right thing. But what is my something?"

A man struggles with observing his friend's affair as he is also close with his friend's wife. Unsure how to respond, he avoids interacting with either and ignores calls and texts from his friend asking for support.

When someone close to you or over whom you have stewardship needs help, notice the stories you tell yourself about what might happen if you get involved. In what ways do these stories serve you? In what ways do they not serve you?

Examining our biases, fears, and Missed Connections is one way forward to understanding what holds us back from empathetically engaging with another.

For people who desire to show up for others yet frequently experience Missed Connection–style interactions, there is good work to be done to examine and expand our empathy and look at the fears that are holding us back. Understanding the Show Up Hard framework can be one step toward greater connection. However, this first book focuses almost exclusively on those of us who tend to become overinvolved.

INTRODUCING THE ENMESHED STYLE OF ENGAGING

"Many of the problems that arise in life are due to our having said 'yes' in situations where we should have said 'no.'"
—Her Holiness Mata Amritanandamayi (Amma)

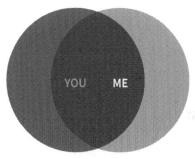

Enmeshed

For many helpers and empaths who are natural givers or higher EQ responders, this second framework is our go-to method of engaging.

At first, engaging in this "all-in" way feels good for both parties involved. Both the person who is in crisis and the person who is helping can feel an initial rush of fulfillment.

In this way, the Enmeshed framework can be tricky.

With time, like an awkward hug gone on too long, the lines become blurred. It is less clear where one person ends and the other begins, less clear whose needs are being met.

The feeling of saving someone or being saved can be a balm for many personality types. This initial impression is confusing, because engaging as Enmeshed is actually the path to burnout and resentment.

When caught up in the Enmeshed framework, you can lose yourself. Being Enmeshed is draining. Simply put, being Enmeshed is not a sustainable way to engage. In the face of overwhelm, we go numb. We lose our ability to show up at all, when Showing Up Hard is what is required to make the change around us. Feeling overwhelmed, bitter, or resentful is a warning sign to check your boundaries. It's highly likely you are operating as Enmeshed.

Synonyms for "enmesh" include words such as ensnare, entangle, entrap, catch, hook, snarl, tangle. Take note of the feelings that come up as you think about those words. What do you notice?

The verb "enable" is defined as giving adequate power, means, or opportunity. So much of the work a helper does is to enable those around them, particularly those with less status or resources, to have greater power, means, or opportunity. Yet the label "enabler" has come to also mean someone who encourages negative or self-destructive behavior in another. Enabling is another aspect through which the Enmeshed role can show up. What begins as an initial good intention can grow to mask our own fear of change, truth speaking, or shining a light on a challenging situation. When "caught," the enabler will feel stuck, as if they are the victim of the situation, as if they have no choice.

NOTE TO SELF

fear is the thief of joy.

Yet the circles framework helps us to take a step back and see another way. As a helper, we own the choices we make. We own communicating clear expectations, readjusting plans, and being completely honest about what we can deliver.

The clues our body gives us can be helpful warning signs. Learning to pay attention to our body can make us aware when we begin to overcommit or slide toward being Enmeshed. Are you working harder than the person you are helping? Yet another clue that the situation is out of balance.

Perhaps you've identified a time you were Enmeshed. Perhaps that time is in a relationship you have right now.

How do you shift an Enmeshed relationship to being one that is defined and more sustainable? Recognizing the situation is the first step. Depending on the circumstances, getting help to make a plan about shifting your engagement may be needed. In some situations, we can have an honest and direct conversation with the person we are involved with and reshape how we engage.

I have a particular knack for overpromising to help people with big ideas, exciting ventures, and worthy projects. I love bringing a big idea into the world. Just the idea of launching something new makes my heart beat faster. I can't tell you the number of mornings I woke up realizing I had, yet again, overpromised to help someone in a way that was not sustainable if I was going to keep up with my other commitments. As a stopgap measure while I was learning to not overpromise in the first place, I would immediately upon realizing my overcommitment write an email or make a phone call and admit my mistake:

I loved meeting you hearing about your big idea. It's an awesome idea and I got excited about thinking how I could be involved.

Truth be told, I'm currently fully committed at work and home and actually can't be helpful. Here is a link to the local resource I mentioned to you.

Wishing you all the best! Can't wait to see you bring this project to life.

Shannon

More recently I've been able to catch myself in the act of overcommitting: "Oh my gosh, I love you and this idea so much. If there were another 24 hours in a day, I would offer to jump on board and help."

To be honest, it took me many years to really embody the fact that I have choice in how I engage. With this realization comes the responsibility of speaking truthfully and directly about my availability. I've had some friend breakups and lost relationships as part of my learning curve to finding more graceful ways to set limits with my inclination to overcommit. Learning has a certain price. Staying Enmeshed has a different price. Finding a support person or people as I navigated these experiences, moving from Enmeshed to a healthier way of engaging, was invaluable.

Some of the most challenging relationships to reconfigure are Enmeshed family relationships. The good news for Enmeshed family relationships is that heaps of professional help is available to aid in getting untangled. See the suggested reading list at the end of the book for ideas on where to get started. In the work setting, support for reimagining a colleague relationship may be available through the human resources department.

Reconfiguring an Enmeshed relationship can be time consuming and painful, though the work is necessary and must be done. Think about it like this: The relationship will ultimately not survive as it is. Something has to shift. Best if you act to shift it in a healthy and thoughtful manner for a better outcome for both parties. Knowing the amount of work involved is all the more reason to figure out how to avoid choosing an Enmeshed framework of engagement in the first place.

INTRODUCING THE COMPASSIONATE WITNESS STYLE OF ENGAGING

"Not all of us can do great things. But we can do small things with great love."

—Mother Teresa

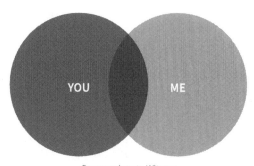

Compassionate Witness

Changing your mind is always an option.

If the Missed Connection style does not create an opening for empathy to be exchanged and support the possibility of creating change and if the Enmeshed style is not sustainable, let's reimagine ourselves in our helper role as a Compassionate Witness. The Compassionate Witness offers themself as an empathetic and perhaps resourceful observer of another's journey. Our goal as a Compassionate Witness is to hold the space for someone and communicate, "I see you. You are not alone."

In the Compassionate Witness framework, it is quite clear where one person begins and the other ends. There is opportunity for profound human connection to occur in the sweet spot where they overlap. As part of that human connection, empathy can be conveyed.

Empathy is a feeling or response directed toward someone else's circumstances or experience. Compassion is an associated feeling that requires you to take positive action to support a person in alleviating their pain or situation. That action is our gift. As a Compassionate Witness, it is our role to show up, to stay steady. As a witness of another's experience, it is not up to us to save them, to define their success, to fix a situation, or even to know the right answers. The Compassionate Witness is not attached to the outcome.

The sweet spot—the space where "you" and "me" overlap—is sacred space where connection occurs. The space between two people matters. Don't approach that space lightly. Honor the opportunity, the invitation, with your thoughtful yes or no. Consider this the zone of maximum possibility—the place where you can offer the very best parts of yourself. The recipe for the sweet spot is a combination of boundaries, vulnerability, and presence mixed with consistency.

After drawing the circles on the overhead projector in the Crisis Hotline volunteer training session, I explained, "In the sweet spot where the circles overlap is the safe zone. We've trained you to show up in this space and talk with callers for fifteen minutes. This framework works. We take 65,000 calls a year based on this model. There are backup clinicians for emergencies and challenging calls. You are not alone. But we don't work outside that sweet spot. The sweet spot is the zone of maximum opportunity, where crisis intervention works. If you want to give out food, go to the food bank. They have a different model for a different crisis—they give out food at designated times each week but do not answer calls 24/7. Or if you want to give a home to someone who is marginally housed, work for Habitat for Humanity. A different model for a different context. This is crisis intervention work, where our mission is to stabilize and refer people to longer-term support that best meets their needs."

Showing up as a Compassionate Witness takes guts, skill, knowledge about what you can offer, clear communication, and awareness throughout the process. It is key that we know ourselves and our empathy journey. We must be keenly aware of how we respond and what our true gifts for creating change are, even if that is simply to listen.

Just like our body can give us clues when our boundaries are off, we can learn to recognize the feeling of being steady and present as a Compassionate Witness. When I encounter a crisis or opportunity to help and am internally preparing to Show Up Hard, I can feel my perceptions sharpen, cluing me in to what is happening around me. As I become mindful of my breathing and the breathing of the person I seek to support, life seems to recalibrate to slow motion. From this place of centeredness and observation, I feel calm inside even as I notice and tally the challenges and opportunities as points of reference for how to best respond. My purpose is aligned with my attention as I assess my availability to support this person for whom I am holding space. Responding as a Compassionate Witness is walking in integrity—being true to our stewardship, our values, and our commitments.

NOTE TO SELF

your love
>
your fear

Explore how the different styles of engaging occur in your life.

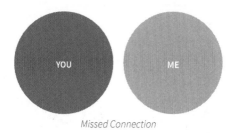

Missed Connection

Reflecting on the Missed Connection framework:

- Describe an interaction when you engaged in this manner.

- Where did you feel the interaction in your body?

- What thoughts did you have?

- In what ways did it serve you?

- In what ways did it serve the other?

- What is your take-away from this reflection?

Enmeshed

Reflecting on the Enmeshed framework:

- Is there a certain person or type of person you frequently become enmeshed with?

- A particular topic you overcommit to with ease?

- What is typically going on for you when you choose to become Enmeshed?

- What are the stories you tell yourself when you engage as Enmeshed?

- Where do you feel an Enmeshed interaction in your body?

- In what ways did being Enmeshed serve you?

- In what ways did it serve the other?

Compassionate Witness

Reflecting on the Compassionate Witness framework:

- Describe an interaction when you engaged as a Compassionate Witness.

- Where did you feel the interaction in your body?

- What thoughts did you have?

- In what ways did it serve you?

- In what ways did it serve the other?

- What is your take-away from this reflection?

2 | PUT YOURSELF ON THE TO-DO LIST

"Caring for myself is not self-indulgence, it is self-preservation. And that is an act of political warfare."

—Audre Lorde

I spent much of my life as a giver. As the oldest of fourteen kids, then in my chosen profession as a social worker, followed by parenting my three children, my orientation to relationships in the world was one of abundant giving. My many privileges, including race, class, education, and resilient emotional makeup, supported this posture of giving, which went on for decades. I'd spent little time consciously considering how I replenished myself. When I unexpectedly divorced and found myself juggling full-time work and solo parenting three small children, I needed to become reacquainted with my inner world and my new relationship to the external world in order to navigate this new landscape. Finding an intimacy with my own desires, beliefs, and preferences was necessary for me to continue to engage with others as a Compassionate Witness. In other words, I needed to know myself to be able to create the boundaries that would allow me to be of service to others. I found myself overall depleted, and some days getting out of bed in the morning felt like a monumental success. I wanted nothing more than to be the giver I had always been and to tap into newfound ambitions for myself, but in order to actualize these dreams, I would need to be able to draw the metaphorical circles of where I began and ended.

On every commercial flight, the flight attendants remind passengers to secure their own oxygen masks first before helping others. Why every single flight? Because our first instinct as a parent or caregiver is to save our child or the person we are looking out for. Rescuing is our natural inclination. The same truth applies in our relationships as helper to those around us. Without our own oxygen mask secured, assuring that we also can breathe, we are of little assistance to others.

With the circles framework as an illustration, we now understand there are various ways we choose to engage and a sustainable way forward as a helper. To Show Up Hard as a Compassionate Witness, consider the yin and yang of giving and receiving. Two opposite forces that, if engaged in balance, give rise to the other. In short, as we learn to both give and receive well, we can do both generously. We know the energy it takes to truly see people and to do so over time, so let's acknowledge what it entails to embody compassion and hold the dark and the light of another's suffering. As a Compassionate Witness, you necessarily commit to replenishing that energy you extend to others. You allow reciprocity for your Compassionate Witness self.

Your desires, wants, and needs also matter. Resource yourself so you can do the emotional labor. As part of the commitment to Show Up Hard, also commit at the outset to a practice of radical self-care, viewed not as a luxury but as a necessity. Self-care is a vital part of the preparation we do to show up and compassionately witness another's journey.

Self-care is the practice of putting yourself on the to-do list. Think about self-care as resourcing yourself, that is, as an investment in your ability to be present and do the hard work, the emotional labor, of compassion. When you commit to self-care, you approach yourself, your schedule, and your life from a place of nurturing. Often, instead of seeing giving and receiving as companions or two parts of a whole, we wait and apply self-care as a reaction to burnout or stress. We wait for the weekend. Or time off. We wait for the kids to grow up. Or for a balanced budget in our program at work. A better practice would be to shift our mindset from self-care as a reaction or an activity that can be put off to seeing this vital practice as an investment in our own resilience. How do you practice self-care?

For me, putting myself on the to-do list and actively seeking that balance between giving and replenishing looks like dedicated time for exercise, meditation, and solitude. In any given week, I can literally find myself on the to-do list through a color-coding system in my calendar. Green is the color I've used to schedule my personal wellness activities. A quick scan of my weekly calendar provides accountability to this commitment to put myself on the to-do list so that I can Show Up Hard for others.

REFLECTION REST STOP

Take a quick mental scan of your week.

- In what ways have you put yourself on the to-do list?

- In what ways would you like to put yourself on the to-do list?

- In an ideal week, what regular self-care activities would be on your calendar?

NOTE TO SELF

you
are
worthy.

3 | LEADING IS A POSTURE

"A leader is best when people barely know he exists, when his work is done, his aim fulfilled, they will say: we did it ourselves."

—Lao Tzu

Challenging times crave change.

View yourself, in your Compassionate Witness role, as an agent of change. Creating change is what is needed at the individual, programmatic, organizational, and societal levels. As a helper extraordinaire, you are well equipped to reimagine yourself in a new role and create the lasting impact you seek to make. Switch from thinking about the job at hand to the role you can play. What if your job is not to be right or knowledgeable; what if your role is to create change?

Leading is a posture of being in the world, a role we assume.

If you

✓ have the potential to guide someone to a better place, or
✓ possess the ability to shine a light on a path ahead, or
✓ consider yourself a steward of the well-being of even one person

—then you are a leader.

You are a steward of creating change. Leaders commit to the emotional labor of showing up to support change. Leaders commit to the long haul of seeing the process of change through.

Leading is both a privilege and a responsibility. Leading is also the responsibility of those with privilege.

A leader is not: a job title, a certain set of skills, a business card, an assignment, or an invitation from someone high up.

The posture of leadership can be adopted by anyone with the guts to believe that change is possible and with the courage to show up.

As you reimagine yourself in a leader role, ask yourself, again: What if your job is not to be right or knowledgeable, but what if your role is to create change?

The Compassionate Witness framework can support us in our leader roles within systems and organizations. We do our work of showing up for others within existing structures, institutions, and cultures. Even values-driven organizations can create unhealthy work environments, whether that looks like a lack of feedback loops for honest appraisal of how work culture aligns with the organization's mission and vision, a commitment to social justice yet not to examining hierarchies within the organization, or insufficient support for frontline staff wellness. Likewise, purpose-driven helpers and managers can struggle in their roles, at times in damaging ways. Take the passive-aggressive boss. Or the manager who fails to examine their own privilege and the impact that lack of self-awareness has on their worldview. Or the person in a position of power who, intentionally or not, relegates the emotional labor to those around them. We all know toxic managers—may we not be one!

Leading is often the work of the everyday and the mundane. Leaders are the people who give the very best parts of themselves without expectation. Imagining oneself as a hero is easy: Fly in and save the day. Showing up when no one is watching, when the stakes are less high, when the task at hand is not as attractive— this is the work of creating change. Showing up is what it takes to lead, to be stewards.

Leaders choose to Show Up Hard. Leaders choose to go first.

NOTE TO SELF

you are a leader.

4 | EMPATHY IS AN ADVENTURE

"Sonder (noun). The realization that each random pass-erby is living a life as vivid and complex as your own—populated with their own ambitions, friends, routines, worries and inherited craziness—an epic story that continues invisibly around you like an anthill sprawl-ing deep underground, with elaborate passageways to thousands of other lives that you'll never know existed, in which you might appear only once, as an extra sipping coffee in the background, as a blur of traffic passing on the highway, as a lighted window at dusk."

—The Dictionary of Obscure Sorrows

Years ago, I began a personal challenge to "stamp my passport," giving myself permission to explore new hobbies, people, and activities with abandon. Just like when I would quickly pop into a nearby country for the passport stamp decades ago as a backpacking student, I again eagerly sought the new and unexplored with delight. Regardless of the outcome of the experience, I had the metaphorical stamp in my passport and ultimately got a crash course in empathy adventures. The permission I gave myself through each challenge gave me the push to overcome fears, have a second look at my assumptions, and stay a little longer than I might have otherwise. No need to force a decision or get my money's worth or any of these other made up constraints I might normally give myself. Because stamp in the passport, baby!

To Show Up Hard as a Compassionate Witness requires being dialed in to empathy. Exploring sonder and being empathetic requires us to go on a journey—to leave the comfort zone of our own narrative and worldview. To step into another's shoes. To see the world through another's eyes and lived experience.

We have expansive experience with empathy from adventuring through characters' experiences in books, movies, and plays. A gifted writer, editor, or producer commits themself to changing the audience with thoughtfully constructed narratives that guide us through the internal worlds of the characters.

Over the doorway as you enter the San Francisco Playhouse is this manifesto:

> *Our theater is an empathy gym where we come to practice our powers of compassion. Here, safe in the dark, we can risk sharing in the lives of the characters. We feel what they feel, fear what they fear, love what they love. And as we walk through these doors we take with us greater powers of understanding to make our community a better place. One play at a time.*

Just as a skilled author, playwright, or screenwriter fully takes on the worldview, persona, and voice of a character to tell the story, as leaders who seek to create change in challenging situations, we, too, can adventure through the narrative of another.

With an empathetic response, we feel connection and an understanding of the other person's feelings or situation; we see the world through their lived experience. With our brain engaged, we are able to truly walk in another's shoes and imagine their story as our own. Being empathetic is a journey beyond developing personas and analyzing storyboards. A shared background or lived experience is not required for this journey. In fact, this is where our true empathy adventures begin. Empathy adventures are an invitation to explore. Empathy adventures are not abstract—they are nuanced, complex, and full of details. Empathy is not synonymous with agreement. In fact, some of the most expansive empathy adventures come from journeys into others' worlds quite opposite our own.

Beginning on an empathy adventure may feel risky, as we leave the comfort of our own worldview and narrative to explore another's. We risk falling in love. We risk feeling deep connection. We risk changing our own mind. We risk returning from this empathy adventure as a different person.

One passport stamping adventure for me was Contact Improvisation dance classes, where I explored the connection between my body, my desires, and my movement in the world. It simultaneously also provided opportunity to connect with my fears and inner critic.

During one class when it was time to choose partners, the feeling from elementary school of being the last chosen for the kickball team emerged from my memory as I scanned the room of already partnered pairs. From my peripheral vision, a person appeared and chose me as if I were the world's greatest partner, not the last to be chosen. We were physically unlikely partners, as my shoulder was near his waist. We initially giggled trying to follow the teacher's instructions to lean into or roll with one another.

It wasn't long before I became lost in our dance, with my eyes closed, until I realized my feet were no longer on the ground and I was moving in the air. A split second later, I'd fallen to the floor. "What happened?" I whispered to my partner.

"You tensed up, and you fell out of the dance. When you let yourself be lifted, you have to let go. You have to trust me," he explained.

"I can't do it. I can trust you when both of my feet are on the ground. But I don't know how to let go and trust you," I said.

Without any judgment, he warmly replied, "That is how you allow yourself to be lifted without falling. If you want to try again, just lean in, and if I feel you trusting, then I'll lift you." Realizing I already knew what it felt like to fall to the mat and that I would be okay, I decided to see what letting go and trusting would feel like. As he lifted me, I opened my eyes. I was being steadily held high, moving through the air, and I could not stop grinning. I felt free. I was flying, literally and figuratively. This is what letting go and trusting feels like!

My passport stamp was the adventure of staying with my fears of not being chosen and of falling to the mat. While there was a physical aspect to the reward—flying through the sky—the adventure was really in my mind: moving through assumptions and old stories to embrace a new opportunity.

The empathy adventure came in talking with my partner after class, when he shared that he was terribly shy. "I can go days without talking to anyone, and longer without being touched by even a handshake. I come to Contact Improv class because I can feel touch," he told me.

NOTE TO SELF

your
vulnerability
is your
greatest
strength.

I realized his keen ability to sense my leaning in and trusting came from well-honed observation skills and appreciation of touch born of loneliness and craving. I think of this man often. When I want to be chosen. Or when I have the opportunity to choose. When I see someone in the world who has a keen sense of observation. Or someone who is shy and quiet. This brief interlude took me on an expansive empathy adventure. Passport stamped, I returned to myself and my life profoundly changed.

How might you stamp your passport by taking empathy adventures? Only you know what is uncharted territory in your own emotional life, but here are a few ideas to get you started on your empathy adventures. Let's see what happens as you head out to explore the new places in your heart.

Take the bus instead of driving. Or walk instead of taking the bus or train.

Go on a walk or run with the goal of getting lost. Leave your phone in your pocket. Using signs, observations, and conversations, find your way back. This one is excellent when arriving in a new city.

Ask someone waiting in the coffee-shop line next to you what they are looking forward to.

Eat a meal with a person who is experiencing homelessness. Ask them about their day and plans for the night.

Ask someone their opinion about a piece of pending legislation, with the only goal to listen and be curious.

Find someone in a different team or department at work and ask them about their weekend plans. Follow up the next week to see how the weekend went.

Find a stranger reading a book. Strike up a conversation about the book, a book they previously read, and what book they are planning to read next.

Volunteer at an event or venue you're not familiar with, such as a film festival, sports event or race, community program, gala event, or food bank. Consider one-off events, which offer ease in popping in and out of another world. Bonus round: Sign up for the least popular activity (clean-up seems to always be available!), where unusual adventures can happen.

Take a class on a skill or topic you are completely unfamiliar with. Activities that ground us in our body are particularly rich adventures. So are book readings or discussion forums on people or topics that we have no expertise on.

As you map your empathy adventures, it's important to recognize the path forward as well as the path back to yourself. The key to being agile, present, and willing to go on empathy adventures is the confidence and assurance you will not become lost (overwhelmed, overcommitted, or in dangerous territory) along the way. For sure, empathy adventures can take us into uncharted territories—this is part of the adventure. Having a strong connection to yourself and being present with your own experience is a piece of your sustainability plan as a Compassionate Witness. Make note of these learnings about going out and returning to yourself by talking with a trusted friend or writing in your journal, providing reinforcement for the next journey.

Make observations of your empathy adventures without judgment. Noticing is an opportunity to develop an intimacy with ourselves. Intimacy with our inner world is what allows us to be increasingly open to others—to be truly empathetic.

Understanding your own empathy adventures is a key step to leading in challenging times, which is a skill you build as you embrace sonder. To know yourself and own your empathy adventures is an act of courage. Awareness of how you respond is a superpower as an empathetic leader.

REFLECTION REST STOP

Recall a recent experience you had with empathy.

• What new territory did this adventure take you to?

• What shifted as you experienced an empathetic response?

• Where did your journey begin?

- Where did your journey end?

- How might you stamp an empathy adventures passport?

- What empathy muscles will you build?

Can't resist? Ready to dive in and go into uncharted empathy territory? Here are several pages for your empathy adventures passport. Set goals for this week or month. Open yourself up to surprise. There are more passport pages to download and print at ShowUpHard.com.

DATE _____

The adventure:

Internal narrative:

Assumption/bias:

What did you notice about your body?

Takeaway:

How I returned to myself:

EMPATHY ADVENTURES PASSPORT

DATE _____

The adventure:

Internal narrative:

Assumption/bias:

What did you notice about your body?

Takeaway:

How I returned to myself:

EMPATHY ADVENTURES PASSPORT

DATE _____

The adventure:

Internal narrative:

Assumption/bias:

What did you notice about your body?

Takeaway:

How I returned to myself:

NOTE TO SELF

Be curious.

5 | SKILLS TO BUILD FOR THE JOURNEY

"We must become the change we want to see."

—Mahatma Gandhi

I received a text message from a colleague asking for advice about a young college-aged friend who was depressed, alone, and potentially suicidal. The start of school was not going well and the friend felt they would not make it through the year.

We understand that empathy is critical to leading, but how can we access empathy when we most need it? Being empathetic is not necessarily a first response. Empathy is a skill that can be learned, developed, and honed. Being empathetic takes energy. Building our empathy muscle begins with noticing.

The practice of lifting weights builds muscle tone, increases the amount of weight you can lift, improves how quickly you can lift weight, and decreases the time it takes to recover after lifting. In a similar fashion, your ability to be empathetic grows with practice. Your capacity for comfort in navigating different settings, opening yourself up to being vulnerable, being present, and returning to yourself following an empathy adventure can expand over your entire lifetime.

Yet, empathy is not a competition. Each of us has our own version of a natural response to a situation where empathy could come into play. To begin building our empathy muscles, we will pay attention to and notice the details and themes of our empathy adventures.

Reflect on the text message from my colleague seeking advice about the student and—without judging your response in any way—determine what your body's response is to this scenario. Where do you feel that response? Write on a piece of paper or say aloud what your body's response would look and feel like if it were to take form.

There are no right or wrong answers. Noticing is the answer.

Now, what is your mind's response to this scenario? What is the story your mind tells you? What does this story remind you of?

Are you drawn closer to this person or situation? Or are you inclined to turn away?

Stay curious.

Noticing our responses simply provides information to help us understand that both our brain and our body respond as we encounter challenging scenarios and opportunities to go on empathy adventures. As a natural reaction to a stressful situation, we have a fight-or-flight response. This response is hardwired thanks to our resilient ancestors of generations past. Which is not to say that empathy adventures are inherently stressful, but rather to acknowledge that the challenge of putting ourselves in new situations and expanding our skill set will inevitably provoke a stress response in our body. The chemical response in our body—or rather, our body's natural response—to a stressful situation is a helpful clue or reminder as to what is going on. Let's reframe this a bit: When faced with an empathy adventure, you might naturally be inclined to engage versus turn away. Our responses are driven both by our internal emotional makeup as well as by our lived experience, including trauma and resilience.

Perhaps your body's response and your mind's response are incongruent. Perhaps they are similar. You can try out different scenarios and see which are softer, which are more triggering for you, and what reminders you observe. Our bodies give us clues, early signs, about what is going on for us in our external and internal worlds. These signs from our body can guide us. Noticing your body's and mind's natural responses builds an awareness of your default or preferred methods of responding. Make observations of your empathy adventures without judgment.

> *As part of a commitment to self-awareness, notice your body's responses to various situations. Where do you first feel the response in your body? How does it feel? In flight mode, how do you feel in your body? In fight mode, how do you feel in your body? In what situations do you feel at ease? The more you can learn to observe your body's responses, the more you can begin to rely on these natural responses as clues. Also be aware of your mind's responses. Do you have a default response to certain situations? What stories come easily to mind? At what speed do the stories in your mind run?*

To close the loop on the story above, the Compassionate Witness response for my colleague (who initially felt scared and too paralyzed to respond) was to go to the friend, so they were no longer alone. After making an assessment that there was no immediate danger, she helped her friend make a plan to get food, water, and return home for a good night's sleep. You'll learn more later in the book about how to craft a container or space for interactions like this.

To return to the metaphor of building physical muscles—I was in a fitness class recently where the instructor coached us, "Slowly rise, slowly rise," as we lifted weights from our waist to our shoulders. The instructor advised this pace was better for our muscles. Such is also true in life. Slowly rise. Rise for the long haul. Rise for the right reason. Don't rush your rising. Slowly rise—aware, observant, present. Slowly rise as you intend to be one who Shows Up Hard for the beginning *and* for the end.

Along with noticing and expanding our empathy muscle, a few additional skills can help us as we Show Up Hard. This is information we likely have learned at some point in life but may have forgotten or not thought to apply in our own Show Up Hard practice. Understanding some basic theory about crisis and conflict can give context to our role as a leader engaging as a Compassionate Witness. Knowing in advance how crisis and conflict impact those around us and our work helps us to prepare.

This theory overview is not meant to alarm you, nor to make you an armchair therapist. Expertise is not required to Show Up Hard. Showing up as we manage others does not require us to go outside our professional skill set. Rather, consider the following overview as guardrails to help guide when and how you engage as well as when to know if outside help is needed.

Let's start with a brief overview of crisis. Crisis is a time-limited response characterized by "a perception or experiencing of an event or situation as an intolerable difficulty exceeding the person's current resources and coping mechanisms." A crisis generally lasts six to eight weeks, during which time the self seeks to re-establish

NOTE TO SELF

slowly
rise.

equilibrium through coping mechanisms.

There are two types of crisis: situational and developmental, both of which generally follow a similar arc toward resolution or homeostasis. The difference between these two is that we can prepare in advance for developmental crisis. Examples of situational crises include accidental death, job loss, and natural disasters. Examples of developmental crises are the birth of a child, retirement, and an adolescent leaving for college.

Grief and loss experiences have their own unique stages of returning to equilibrium: Denial, anger, bargaining, depression, and acceptance. Often, similar stages or cycles are seen as we grapple with integrating other situational or developmental crisis experiences into our new state of equilibrium.

At the beginning of a crisis it is hard to imagine ever returning to "normal" or equilibrium—the crisis state feels too overwhelming and disruptive. When we are experiencing a state of crisis, being gently reminded that life will not always be like this moment can be helpful in reframing the experience. Life may get worse or it may get better, but change is inevitable. In fact, we will never return to "normal," but we will return to a state of equilibrium—the body will regulate itself to this state. This is both the danger and opportunity of crisis: the chance for profound change to occur.

When experiencing crisis, we naturally begin to regulate using coping mechanisms. The goal of coping mechanisms is to help us return to a place of balance or equilibrium. Coping mechanisms are on a spectrum from healthy to unhealthy. Healthy coping mechanisms include going on a run, writing in a journal, taking a bath, meditating, and petting a dog. Unhealthy coping mechanisms include blaming others, lashing out verbally, violence toward ourselves or others, and activities that are addictive.

You might recall a crisis event in the life of someone close to you in which they emerged triumphant or as a better person. This person may even sing the praises of the crisis for bringing them to this new place of being. You might also know someone who emerged from a crisis with a new equilibrium less functional or more chaotic than before the crisis event. Our upbringing, connection in community, prior coping mechanisms, innate resiliency and any privilege (race, gender, class) all play roles in the ultimate outcome.

As a society, we are fixated on the hero's journey, the triumphant phoenix rising from the ashes. While this is not the space to explore that myth, suffice it to say that bringing judgment to the Compassionate Witness journey will not serve you as an empathetic leader. How someone emerges from a crisis is their journey and their narrative. Our role as a leader is to show up and to be aware of the circumstances.

Our goal as a leader is to recognize, if not plan for, crisis for ourselves and those around us, to encourage healthy or healthier coping mechanisms, and to stabilize people in the moment of crisis. It is the role of first responders, crisis hotlines, therapists, doctors, and other healers to do the work of crisis response. Healing and full integration of crisis experiences takes time—and there is not an expiration date on that process.

As a leader, we choose the role of noticing and doing the brave work of showing up.

Now, let's explore an overview of conflict. Conflict occurs when people have varying views, a difference in beliefs or opinions, or their desired outcomes seem incompatible. Conflict is a part of life and can be expected in management roles. Common methods for dealing with conflict include avoidance, accommodation, collaboration, compromise, and competition. Most people use all or most of these methods, with their response varying by situation. We generally have more common methods we default to. It is worth noting that a method or style is not a silo or label for a person, but it is rather indicative of a coping mechanism or response that has served them well previously.

An effective leader understands their own default response to conflict. Effective leaders do not operate at the extremes and can transition between styles in the middle. Effective leaders notice the styles used by people in their stewardship. Developing plans to resolve conflict can go a long way toward a timely resolution that satisfies all parties. Preparing can help us be less guarded and more present. A wise helper will see conflict, acknowledge the conflict, and make plans for resolving the conflict.

COMMON METHODS FOR DEALING WITH CONFLICT

avoidance	collaboration	competition
accommodation		compromise

Less talking and more listening never hurts. Listening skills are definitely worth investing in.

When I was a young social worker doing my field placement in a New Orleans housing project, my field supervisor tasked me with recording a session with a client, with their permission, and transcribing that session for our next supervision meeting. As an intern, I worked in a program supporting families at risk of losing a child to family services. We provided parenting classes, home visits, and counseling sessions and linked parents with community resources. I chose to record a client session with a woman I felt particularly connected to. I wanted to showcase my best skills to my supervisor.

After the recorded session, I sat at home in front of my typewriter and began the slow process of listening to a sentence on the tape recorder, pressing stop, typing that sentence, repeating. As the words began to appear on the page, I was horrified to see how many words came from my mouth. I cringed each time I pushed play on the tape recorder and heard more of myself talking. There was a part of me that wanted to cheat and not transcribe all that I had said. I felt embarrassed by the pages documenting the sheer volume of my words as well as the content: waxing eloquent about theory, offering unsolicited parenting advice, asking leading questions.

I took the full transcript to my next supervision session and handed it to my supervisor: "I'm so embarrassed. I wished I had time to record another session, to do it again. I feel ashamed of how much I talked." My supervisor glanced over the pages. In her typical calm and wise manner, she reflected, "That is an awful lot of talking." I agreed. She asked why I'd talked so much. I shared my desire to do a good job, to highlight my learnings from school, to win her praise, and to be considered smart. "I notice your why had nothing to do with the client and what she wanted or needed." I agreed. Boom! This is a truth I will never forget.

My supervisor handed the transcript back and told me to do it again. I returned to the client, apologized for the previous session, and explained why I had talked so much. I asked permission to try again. She agreed. This time when I pressed the record button, I was cognizant of each word that came out of my mouth, wondering what it would feel like to type every letter onto the page. This awareness forced an opportunity to sit, however comfortably, with silence and wait for the client to respond. With less talking, I became more aware of my body's posture and the energy I brought to the interaction. I had more attention for the client and her words because I spent less energy in my mind formulating what I would say next. In fact, there was less pressure overall, as I did not need to know so much or appear witty or wise.

After I typed up this second session, I saw there were fewer words in general, as there had been periods of silence. There were rich details of the client's life and bits of progress on her journey, even in this one session. I was nearly invisible on paper. I could have been anyone. Anyone who was listening, that is.

Listening is, in fact, a job all its own.

A baseline understanding of crisis, coping skills, and conflict supports us as a leader in choosing how to respond and understanding the responses of others. Building and refining our empathy, noticing, and listening skills can be a practice for our lifetime. Taking the skills you have on hand now and applying them to the Show Up Hard framework will amplify your ability to be a Compassionate Witness. Whether at home or work and a need arises, I return again and again to these basic understandings and skills to help frame my plan for the best way forward.

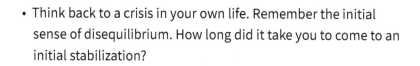

- Think back to a crisis in your own life. Remember the initial sense of disequilibrium. How long did it take you to come to an initial stabilization?

- What did further stabilization look like?

- What factors were key in supporting a sense of well-being?

- What are your favorite coping mechanisms? Which are healthy? Which are less healthy?

- As a leader, what coping mechanisms can you proactively support in the culture around you?

- What are your preferred methods of dealing with conflict?

- How are they different at home, work, in person, and online?

- What methods of dealing with conflict do you fear the most? Why?

NOTE TO SELF

Notice.

6 | EMBARK BEFORE YOU ARE READY

"There is a crack in everything. That's how the light gets in."
—Leonard Cohen

My friend Julia's empathy adventure began with an evening photography class at the community college. She'd received a camera from her parents for her birthday. With a goal to start a photo blog showcasing her new hobby, she offered to take pictures of people in the neighborhood, ask them questions about their connection to the location, and write a short piece to accompany their photo on her blog. While she had expected to hone her photography skills and connect with new people, her experience quickly became one of deeper connection and sondor. She called me one night several weeks into her project: "I'm not sure I can keep doing this. I think I need to be a trained therapist. Sometimes people tell me such hard stories. While they don't ask for help, I feel like I am not qualified to do this." "Qualified to take photos, to listen, to provide a space for people to share their stories?" I asked her. She paused. We reviewed the skills she had for empathy: Her ability to notice, her commitment to listening, and her baseline knowledge of crisis and conflict.

In fact, Julia was ready. In fact, sonder was happening as Julia showed up as a Compassionate Witness.

Opportunities to Show Up Hard come to us whether we are "ready" or not. We don't need to be completely healed or professionally trained to be a Compassionate Witness. Sometimes I see people holding back, Missed Connection–style, believing they have to be perfect or better in order to show up for others. While perfection is not required, we do need a practice of centering ourselves; this is the core of the Compassionate Witness framework. Centering ourselves is also needed for our own healing, but that is another book with different goals and outcomes.

Ultimately, we need to be fully human to connect with another. Being fully human means we Show Up Hard with our scars and flaws. As we go on more and more empathy adventures, we often choose to reclaim our traumas and build resilience as we become increasingly aware of our own empathy journeys. Knowing yourself enough and choosing to get help from a trained therapist, trusted confidant, or inspired coach is a sign of strength. Being compassionate to ourselves is a key part of being able to show up for others.

Your secret sauce, the one that allows to you enter the space where you will make magic as you show up as a Compassionate Witness for others, is a mix of vulnerability, consistency, and presence. If you know yourself and your tendencies during empathy adventures, you can commit to protecting the tender parts of yourself as you Show Up Hard. This protection acts as a buffer against feeling ragged. Your vulnerable self is worth protecting.

You are enough. If I could, I would come into your house at night and paint this phrase on your bathroom mirror. That way, you'd see the message morning and night as you brushed your teeth and combed your hair. Maybe after reading it over and over, this message would sink into your memory and become part of your truths, something you never doubted. You are enough.

Of course, you are going places. I know you have major dreams, epic goals, and a long to-do list. But know this: You are enough. Just as you are, right now, in this very moment, you are enough.

Yes, there are times you cry in the shower so no one will know. Yes, some mornings you wake up and stare out into the blank new day thinking you should've stay curled up in bed. Even then, you are enough. Tell yourself. Over and over. You are enough.

You are moving down your path in life—maybe you skip, perhaps you dance, sometimes you might even do the backward walk. There are times you will stop on your path to smell the flowers or examine the hole in the ground; that's just how going down your path works. It does not matter how you go, but go you will.

However you are traveling down your path, please smile the smile of someone who knows that they are enough.

You are enough.

Find your place of enoughness. Go there often. You arrive at the sweet spot of the Compassionate Witness from your place of enoughness. In your place of enoughness, you are full and at ease. There is a lack of want or entitlement. There is a lightness yet purpose to how you face the world. Your curiosity piques with ease. You do not feel competitive.

To find my place of enoughness, I travel through all my fears and shame, leaving behind what will not serve me in this interaction, to arrive in the sweet spot and see the other person. In my place of enoughness, there is an absence of longing and an ease to my generosity. I am whole, walking in integrity, and ready to serve the greater good. I bow to you in the sweet spot as a humble warrior.

NOTE TO SELF

you
are
enough.

BOOK TWO

Detours

Some of the best memories we make along road trips come from the unexpected detours. We've all been lost, missed the turn, even run out of gas. Once my sister was driving and we were so busy chatting, she turned onto the freeway going the wrong direction! We laugh ourselves silly every time we remember how she quickly and safely recovered this error.

While I'm all for making memories, there are some common detours we encounter as empathetic leaders that are too painful to take. Detours can lead to burnout—I know from personal experience. While we'll certainly strive to enjoy the journey and embrace opportunities for lessons learned, we can proactively avoid detours with advanced warning and equipped with some additional skills for our Compassionate Witness framework.

1 | CONFUSING LEADING WITH SAVING

Your deep desire, perhaps even your magnificent capacity, for helping others finds you smack dab in the middle of Enmeshed relationships as you try to support others at work and in your community.

Leaders are in the role of supporting change, embracing a posture of forward motion. Maybe you observe someone in crisis, and your immediate response is to save them or to believe they "need" healing. Indeed, perhaps the person in crisis wants to be healed or saved. But don't confuse leading with healing or saving others. Even for leaders who are trained as healers, be clear about your role. Leaders show up as a Compassionate Witness and offer resources or referrals that could lead to healing. The goal of the leader is to create the change by holding steady in the face of overwhelming and uncertain situations. Healing work is best done by trained professionals. Leading is subtle, present, and sustainable. Be clear on what your role is. And is not.

When crises or challenging situations present themselves and we are in a position to lead, we can be tempted by the seductive flirt of the idea that we might save someone. This temptation is a dangerous detour from the Compassionate Witness path. Even when our intentions are good, our ego can be seduced by an idea that is not actually true. I am in a frequent dance with my ego. It is a strong, persistent, and ambitious voice that provides regular commentary on my day-to-day life. I have mad respect for, and walk closely with, my ego for the strength and fortitude to carry forward in daily life.

That said, I often need to metaphorically shake hands with my ego and say, "Ease up, sister!"

Some signs that pop up for me indicating I need to pause and check in with myself are:

- ✓ Any dynamic I've created where I believe I am saving someone.
- ✓ I believe I am the only one who can be there for this person.
- ✓ I've created a sense of self-imposed urgency.
- ✓ I'm working harder than the person I am helping.
- ✓ I believe there is a reward for me at the end.

Whenever I find myself on such a detour, I pause to have a conversation with my ego. It goes something like this:

Hello, Ego!

Good to see you again.

You do a lot of hard work. I want to give you a break around one topic—saving people. You've never saved anyone. You never will. It's not possible.

A human being saves themself.

We might tell ourselves a story that we are saving lives or we saved a person. Sure, that story feels good. In reality, we created a structure or provided resources or changed the environment so someone could save themself.

Mad respect and always with you,

Shannon

It's critical to understand this point, because being unattached to the outcome is essential for a Compassionate Witness.

Three reasons for this position:

1. People save themselves. This is a truth.

2. By being attached to what will eventually happen or to a particular outcome as a helper, we inadvertently limit the potentially stunning possibilities with our own limited thinking, beliefs, or knowledge. Allowing the journey to unfold exactly as it should creates space for magic, for possibilities beyond our imagination, and for the person's own truth to come into being.

3. If we are attached to the good outcomes, we also necessarily need to be attached to the less fortunate outcomes. It's only fair. And that sucks. Not only does it suck—it is not true. We do not create bad outcomes for people. Just like we don't save people.

Understanding this at a deep level is freeing. It allows you to show up as a Compassionate Witness even when you don't know the right answer or best choice. Perhaps this is an even better place to arrive from.

As a compassionate and resourceful observer of another's journey, you can witness their own story unfolding. This gentle, steady observation is a gift beyond anything you could actually give to someone.

Get comfortable looking uncertainty in the eye and staying present with what is. Your presence is your greatest offering.

NOTE TO SELF

Park
your
ego.

2 | ARE YOUR NARRATIVES YOUR IDENTITY?

"Compassion is not a relationship between the healer and the wounded. It's a relationship between equals. Only when we know our own darkness well can we be present with the darkness of others. Compassion becomes real when we recognize our shared humanity."

—Pema Chödrön

You are Showing Up Hard, yet find yourself stuck in a roundabout in your own head—leaving you unable to move forward to the next level. The volume of the story you tell yourself is turned up to 11. I get it. It happens to me, too.

We each arrive to empathy adventures with stories born of our lived experience. Just as the Crisis Hotline training asked volunteers to explore their why behind coming to do this work, it is useful for you to explore your why. Why do you show up? Understanding what brings us to this work and what will sustain us truly matters as we Show Up Hard.

Part of the magic of empathy adventures is the opportunity to grapple with our own narrative as we begin on the adventure of exploring another's worldview.

Some of our stories, some narratives, are particularly sticky. I call them sticky stories. These narratives are created from experiences of trauma and crisis that are not yet integrated or fully healed. Stories born in watershed moments can attach themselves to our identity and innate responses, becoming sticky stories. We become stuck, unable to reframe the story or how we respond.

I know firsthand the stunted path of holding onto a narrative that no longer serves oneself. For years, I carried the story of my divorce trauma beyond its expiration date. Though the story no longer served me, its sticky factor meant it clung. With hardly a moment's notice when something emotional appeared on the horizon, this sticky and tired story would emerge. At the very end of this story's exhausted days, I had the awareness to notice that the old narrative had become like a favorite pet I would pat whenever change or uncertainty was on the horizon. To fully integrate the experience and reframe the narrative required healing—important work I did with a gifted therapist. Integrating the previously sticky story allowed me to face challenges with a new narrative.

Perhaps you can identify a story around leadership and helping imprinted on you decades ago, or themes related to how you sustain this work that may or may not be true, or a story based on fear creating a limitation in your ability to Show Up Hard. When in doubt or feeling stuck, don't hesitate to give the past a break. If even for a few minutes, an hour, or an afternoon. You can always return to that particular story after allowing it a break from the exhausting task of running through your mind.

Releasing what no longer serves us is part of the brave and courageous work we do to create change within ourselves or others. Hoping for a better past is like driving full speed ahead while only looking in the rearview mirror.

Narrative becomes identity.

As a leader who understands the power of empathy in the relationships around you, your first step is to understand your own stories, triggers, and responses. The next step is to recognize the role narratives, triggers, and responses play in those we seek to serve. Remember that others' responses are not about you. That sticky story is theirs. But seeing the sticky story for what it is allows you to meet them in the sweet spot as a Compassionate Witness with more clarity.

For example, Marta, a manager of a team of peer advocates, observed one staff member was consistently prickly about timing. Commitments taking longer than expected or meetings not starting on time elicited a large response from Alyssa. During a one-on-one, Marta took the opportunity to note this: "Alyssa, I notice it is challenging for you when people do not stick to the timeline and extensions are made. Or when I am running late and our sessions don't start on time."

Alyssa looked down at her hands as she shared a brief story from her childhood. She didn't have as much time with her father as she would have liked. When they did have time, her dad struggled with communication and picking her up from her activities on time. Ever since, she has kept a close eye on who keeps their promises and who makes her wait.

While it is not up to us to decide, one wonders if this story about timekeeping ultimately still serves Alyssa. Marta recognized this sticky story from Alyssa's childhood was not about Marta, and nor was it Marta's to fix. That said, as a Compassionate Witness, she could clearly see how juggling her own calendar under the impression Alyssa could wait had set into motion a sticky story that was not serving the greater good of the work they had to do together.

Knowing this, Marta responded, "Thank you for trusting me with your story. Alyssa, our time together means a lot to me. I will commit to watching the clock and setting an alarm so we always meet on time. And you are welcome to knock on the door or otherwise bring it up when I do not. Let's keep talking about how to support you when the team needs to make an extension to a timeline. We are here for you."

Even if Alyssa hadn't shared her story or been aware of the connection between her current behavior and the details from her childhood, Marta might have been curious: "I wonder what attachment Alyssa has to timing? What has happened?" Noting others' sticky stories allows us to see their whole selves and at the same time create a distance from that story being our responsibility, which allows us to hold space for them.

Consider stories in your own life that no longer serve you. Perhaps you've grown, matured, learned new skills, or moved on. Write down this favorite story, old and tired as it is. Identify the clues you've noticed as to why carrying it around has become uncomfortable, why it no longer fits. Then think about what your new true story is. If you have not yet arrived at the new true story, imagine what might be next, what you desire.

Crafting our internal identity through narrative is powerful and important work. Understanding the stories we carry with us and the role they play in our responses to experiences around us is a vital part of being able to Show Up Hard for others.

Narrative becomes identity. Own yours.

I do this exercise frequently, sometimes even tearing off the stories that no longer serve me along with their accompanying clues and burning them in a ritual, as a proper farewell. Honoring and giving thanks to a narrative that carried me for months or years allows it to be released and free, creating an opening for a new story and for possibility. Take some time to journal here about one of your sticky stories. There are additional sticky story worksheets to download and print at ShowUpHard.com.

• Stories that no longer serve me. Sticky. Old. Tired.

- Clues the story no longer fits. What is uncomfortable?

- New true stories. What is next? What do I desire?

NOTE TO SELF

Give
the past
a break.

3 | EMPATHY IS NOT SYMPATHY

Upon hearing of an untimely death in a colleague's family, I noticed my response was somewhat flat and entirely inactive. After noticing my response was not as empathetic as I would have liked, I became curious as to how I might still open up possibilities to respond as a Compassionate Witness. To connect with others and to create change, we must traverse the chasm between sympathy and empathy. While I felt sorry about or toward this family's loss, I did not feel empathy, blocking my capacity for the compassion and emotional labor needed to Show Up Hard.

Empathy and sympathy are often incorrectly used interchangeably. While sympathy can be a start on the path toward empathy and true connection, a leader recognizes sympathy is not enough. While we won't judge ourselves or others who are at the sympathy stage, as we seek to make change, we'll recognize the stunted engagement a sympathy posture brings.

With sympathy, we have not placed ourselves in the other's shoes. Sympathy lacks connection. The sorrow or pity that is sympathy may be experienced as looking down on the other's distress or pain. Sympathy may be guarded and a way to hold back. Sympathy may be self-serving. Sympathy is summoned from a place of pity rather than true understanding of the other.

Empathy takes a different level of energy and engagement, a commitment to showing up. Empathy is more powerful than sympathy and is at the core of the Show Up Hard practice. To bypass or overcome a sympathy response we do the requisite emotional labor to engage from a place of empathy. As leaders we have made a commitment to do the emotional labor required to Show Up Hard. A challenging situation or crisis is more than a complex problem for our brain to solve. In fact, challenging situations are more often a complex emotional puzzle, with each emotional puzzle piece playing a role and requiring effort to truly see.

Emotional labor is the unseen and often unacknowledged work that is required to examine what it will take to traverse the chasm between sympathy and empathy. Through emotional labor, we can observe both our own response as well as see the world through the other's eyes. While we can build our skill at doing emotional labor, it is not a step that can be overlooked, however quickly we may be able to do it in some situations. Emotional labor is the gift we offer another as we choose to Show Up Hard in our desire to support forward motion. Emotional labor is a valuable part of what we offer when we chose to be of service to others.

When individuals, teams, and programs begin to grapple with integrating empathy into their ethos, I often notice the overuse of the phrase "I'm sorry." It's the prescriptive phrase to connection in the customer service world. The abundance of "I'm sorry" in online chats (with humans or bots), toll-free phone calls, and email exchanges is almost humorous, except for how frustrating it is. "Are you really sorry?" I often wonder. Because if they were truly sorry, then why don't they change things? If "I'm sorry" is not part of an apology with the goal of making amends, then it is sympathy and not empathy. Likewise, I often see women saying "I'm sorry" for activities that essentially amount to them taking up space in the world or trying to do their jobs. What's it for? At this point. "I'm sorry" has little meaning for me in my Show Up Hard work. When I'm not paying attention or I'm going through the motions of showing up, I find myself slipping, and a hollow "I'm sorry" passes my lips, when in fact my true presence without any words would have been a greater gift. I try to avoid "I'm sorry," except for the frequent times I need to apologize for being wrong. "I'm sorry" then is freely and thoughtfully given as an apology and part of my making amends.

SYMPATHY
(note the distance)

EMPATHY
(note the proximity)

I see you, wouldn't want to be you.
You are really suffering. This is so hard.

I feel so sorry for the homeless. How bad would it to be to not have the motivation to get a job or want to better yourself.
I'm curious where people experiencing homelessness were before the street. I wonder what they dream about at night.

I just can't imagine what you are going through.
You never expected this. It's overwhelming.

I'm so sorry.
I don't have words. This is so much.

During one particularly challenging period of parenting, I kept the details of what was happening close, as sharing would necessarily disclose others' stories. As the toll of these challenges began to add up, I sometimes out of necessity shared pieces with people in my immediate world. There was no shortage of sympathy. Most people were truly sorry for me and for this challenge—ever grateful to not be walking in my shoes. The only thing less helpful than someone feeling sorry for me was unsolicited advice, a freebie sympathetic people often have on hand, which they give as a way to make themselves feel like they have done something. Often, sympathetic responses left me with a desire to retreat further.

After months of the extreme highs and lows that accompany such a learning curve, I had the opportunity to see a colleague I'd not been in touch with for over a year. "You've been quiet for a while, and I haven't seen you around. How are you really doing?" she inquired. I told her the truth. She saw my struggle, my pain, my fear. She held the entirety of it without feeling sorry for me. Rather she held me and my family's story with warm regard for our strength and the sheer beauty of the extremes these kinds of challenges can bring. She saw my journey and observed it to be exquisite. A few days later I received a card in the mail from her. The words traveling across the country through the postal system carried a special weight, knowing the envelope had been passed hand to hand to reach me. "I wish you strength, love for yourself, and continuing to be the beautiful person that you are." This empathetic response was the balm of sonder bridging my struggles at home with my work world.

Another detour that keeps us stuck in Sympathy Land when we aim to be empathetic is holding too tightly to our own belief system. Even with our best efforts to connect with empathy, we'll be held back within our own worldview if we're gripped white-knuckled to our own story or beliefs. Loosening ever so slightly the death hold on our own belief system creates opportunity for movement toward empathy.

I fully learned the value of turning the world upside down and considering that I might be wrong as a way to loosen my grip on a belief system that kept empathy at bay. It began on a playground in a new-to-me neighborhood as we searched for a sports team for my then eight-year-old to join. This phase of life was tightly packed and somewhat precariously put together, like a Jenga game that has gone on for days. I frequently felt overwhelmed and behind.

As we waited for the coach's break so we could inquire about openings on the team, my boys and I started playing on the play ground jungle gym. I showed off my grade school monkey bar skills and, with delight, I hung upside down from the bar, swinging from my bent knees, my hair brushing the sand as I swung like a pendulum back and forth. I could feel my grin upside down, noticing the strangeness of the corners of my mouth pulled toward the earth rather than away. The sounds of parents and children playing around me were familiar, but being upside down, I couldn't recognize anything—everything just looked like unrecognizable shapes of color with shadows, and the sounds I heard didn't seem to attach to any of these moving shapes. It was the same overwhelming world, but upside down, I was detached from my own sense of reality enough to truly see: patches of sunlight, shadows in the shape of a child chasing an adult, the sound of a toddler trying to reach the swing, the feel of my sons nearby. I thought to myself, "Hey, this world looks just right, not so overwhelming. There are simply pieces of experiences around me I can put together to form any truth I choose." Was it the blood rush to my head or a brief encounter with enlightenment? What if I was wrong in how I'd constructed a belief system about my current situation?

It turns out that thinking I might be wrong is one of my best tricks for Showing Up Hard and a fast track to Empathy Land. I take my strongest beliefs and turn them upside down to see what shakes out. Seething with anger, jealousy, tears, fear—any of my dark-side feelings—is a sure reminder to see if I can flip the story in my head upside down and think, even for a moment, that I might be wrong. Often, at least one opportunity will fall out of this experiment. And generally, I can then see my feelings as the shapes and colors they are, rather than the marching orders they give.

At times we are not able to extend our empathy until we embrace an opportunity to grow. I often think about these people or experiences as opportunities to "bow to the Buddha" within each person or experience. In Buddhism we bow to the Buddha with gratitude for the teaching and wisdom. What happens when we use that same frame of mind on incredibly frustrating people or situations? Meaning, a person can be so frustrating, the situation so impossible, the time in life so overwhelming that we instinctively rage against it rather than simply bow to the opportunity within. Raging against it will attract more of the same and offer power to that very thing we want to become smaller or less overwhelming. Bowing to the Buddha inside that person or moment allows us to soften internally, not hold so tightly to the stories we've assigned to certain shapes and shadows, and perhaps put the story together in a new way that's better suited for growth, progress, and our walk toward empathy.

If you are experiencing a sympathy detour on your journey, return to the tools we learned in the "Empathy Is An Adventure" chapter in Book 1 as a compass to reorient yourself to the Compassionate Witness path. Whenever I arrive as my sympathetic self on the scene of an opportunity to Show Up Hard, I pause to notice. And then I begin on my empathy adventure.

Think
that you
might be
wrong.

4 | TUNNELS

"It is only with the heart that one can see rightly; what is essential is invisible to the eye."

—Antoine de Saint-Exupéry

It's the middle of the night and I've woken up. My fears have a field day in the dark and aloneness of the night. I find myself deep in a doomsday scenario based on a mere one or two actual facts from my daytime life. The quietness of the hour magnifies the extremes until I try to force progress by choosing between two unattractive choices. Do we stay or do we go?

While the middle of the night is not particularly friendly for my personal grappling with black-and-white thinking, tunnel vision is a detour that in fact thrives just as well during the day. Often when we are under pressure from conflict, trauma, or crisis, we develop tunnel vision, by which we see fewer rather than more options. Tunnel vision—black-and-white thinking—is painful. In this place we feel stuck.

When you observe someone who is feeling stuck or seeing life through tunnel vision, it is an act of generosity to brainstorm options with them. Support them in expanding their tunnel vision to see three or more options, getting off the either/or dynamic.

What happens when you jump off the binary and wildly explore possibilities? Can you brainstorm twenty options? Might you even have a laugh in the process? What happens when you list crazy, wild, or forbidden choices?

Even this bit of freedom that arrives with more options can give the space for people to move themselves forward.

It is an empowering experience to feel like we have a choice rather than like life has been chosen for us and it is do/die, either/or.

Tunnel vision is in its most acute form and can be clearly seen when someone is suicidal. The suicidal person believes they have two choices:

1. Die.

2. Continue to live with this level of pain and suffering.

When talking with someone who is suicidal, counselors and trained crisis hotline volunteers work to help the person expand the options available to them. To be clear, dying is never not one of the options. That is the person's choice (regardless of our moral beliefs or local laws). It's not worth the energy arguing about the choice to die, as it challenges the fundamental autonomy of the person—which is not an argument you want to lose.

Instead, the person helping focuses on expanding the other options on the table. The vantage point of the person who is suffering, their black-and-white thinking, begins to make sense when we go on an empathy adventure to understand their pain. So, we do the emotional labor of engaging so we can help brainstorm additional options with the goal of finding at least one that is viable for the immediate future. We ask: "What would it look like to live but have less pain and suffering? If life for the next week, or day, had less pain and suffering, what would that look like?" Perhaps the person suggests sleeping through the night would alleviate some of their suffering. Immediately you have a third option on the table—get more sleep—as a potential solution for less suffering. Then we ask: "What support do you need? What needs to change for you to sleep through just one night?" A good night's sleep will yield a slightly different view of the world and likely less suffering, offering a better place from which to reassess the existing option.

A third option shifts the binary tunnel vision in a way that will very likely illuminate additional options, presenting themselves as the next adjacent possibility. Expanding tunnel vision is a small step toward altering the future, with the control being in the hands of the person who makes the decisions. Rather than devising a grand, heroic plan to save the day, the true work of changing lives is in providing the support for someone to make these small steps to expand their options.

Let's try on a different situation. One of the longtime frontline staff in your program, Luis, is struggling to stay focused at work, with frequent calls from his daughter, Maria. His daughter sees her only choice as being to quit high school. It's a black-and-white decision for her, leaning heavily toward quitting. Why? The only other option she sees is staying in school, where she feels unseen, uninterested in the material, and miserable with her social life. It's not hard to see where she's coming from. I'd want to quit, too. After you talk through options with Luis for getting through this stuckness, he makes some dad-and-me time with his teen. He brings some drinks and snacks (snacks are always excellent additions to a brainstorming session!) and sits down with Maria to come up with as many options as possible. "I'd love to sit with you for just 10 minutes. Let's brainstorm as many ideas as we can. I'll bet we can come up with 20. Let's go!"

Ideally, Maria writes down the options, but Luis might help just to get the process going. Writing the options on sticky notes or index cards can help with sorting or stacking them afterward. But don't let supplies get in the way. I've done many a brainstorm on the inside of a cut-open paper grocery bag or papers pulled from the recycling bin at work. To begin the brainstorming, Luis adds "Quit high school" as a prominent option. He doesn't deny this option or take it away. He also adds "Stay miserable and finish high school." There are now two unattractive options on the table. At the start of the process, Luis also set a timer to give a clear start and end to the brainstorm, making sure within the first few minutes of the sprint Maria is offering as many or more ideas than he is. When the timer goes off, they have:

1. Move to Australia (*Alexander and the Terrible, Horrible, No Good, Very Bad Day* reference—generally cracks a smile).

2. Get a general education diploma (GED).

3. Enroll in online high school.

4. Transfer to a school in a different neighborhood.

5. Transfer to a school in the next town.

6. Stay with relatives in a different city for a year and attend high school there.

7. Quit math class (the worst of all the classes for Maria) and take this course at community college.

8. Switch to a different math class with a different teacher.

9. Make a new friend.

10. Join a sport or club (to shift the social dynamic even slightly).

11. Get an after-school job.

12. Talk with the school counselor to see how other youth have dealt with similar problems.

13. Explore options for finishing high school with community college classes.

14. Explore meditation or other mindfulness practices to deal with annoyances.

15. Have a meeting with a teacher to explain the curriculum does not feel relevant and find out what can be done.

16. Talk with the school counselor to see if there is a different set of classes to take to graduate.

17. Find out if it's possible to graduate sooner—meaning fewer classes at high school and additional classes at community college.

18. Investigate what summer school options are available to make up for the particular classes that are too miserable to complete this year.

19. Identify a class that would be interesting to take; figure out how to switch to that class, or enroll in one at community college in exchange for continuing the less–attractive class at high school.

20. Volunteer for a community program that involves a topic of interest.

Luis and Maria now spread out the ideas across the table. A heap of these ideas Maria might not love, of course. Even in the absurd and laughable we can find options, though they are choices we may not ultimately opt for. But in looking at a brainstorm like this, Maria can see possibility rather than a black-and-white choice. Luis tells her, "So, quitting is still an option. But I wonder what it looks like to put that decision off for a week while you explore one or two of these other options. I saw you light up when we talked about a class at community college. Tell me more."

At this point, Maria has more of a journey than a do-or-die situation in front of her. It's not going to be easy, of course. Luis may need to have this conversation multiple times. Each time, the practice of illuminating choices and finding movement from the stuck feeling of tunnel vision is a gift.

Volume is key. A few absurd or outrageous ideas always help shift the dynamic: "If you could wave a magic wand and solve X, what would that look like?" When brainstorming, a few outlandish ideas can jiggle our brain into identifying some smaller ideas, making baby steps toward an adjacent possibility. The outlandish ideas come with associated feelings of freedom or relief, which help to identify what is behind the stuckness. Knowing what feels freeing or what brings relief will lubricate the brainstorming of options that provide similar, if less dramatic, senses of the same.

How might you apply this technique to the tunnel vision of the below situations:

✓ A staff member you supervise has made a clumsy yet large mistake and sees their options as: quitting today before anyone notices or being caught and feeling publicly humiliated.

✓ A friend's partner has betrayed them, and they feel like their options are: throwing the partner out tonight or staying with them long term and feeling small and bitter.

✓ Two extended family members who do not get along see their only options as: a total showdown or never attending the same family event ever again.

✓ Your own black-and-white thinking, wherever and however it emerges.

One of the original either/or options may still be chosen in the end. Or, more accurately, a version of the original option may be chosen. However, the choice will not be made from the tunnel vision place of stuckness. There will be more nuance to the option and a sense of autonomy in choosing, rather than feeling like there is no choice involved in the matter.

Active listening and asking open-ended questions is key to the work we do with someone as they expand their view from tunnel vision. Listening does not require us to solve the problem or situation at hand. Rather, active listening can be a huge, if not the most important, part of showing up for another. Open-ended questions can clarify the scope and magnitude of a situation, giving clues to what has happened and how the person may be triggered based on their lived experience. Of course, we receive this information without judgment.

Your words, pace, and posture are part of the "language" you use to communicate you are present and paying attention. Become aware of how you can shift your words, pace, and posture in different scenarios to reflect varying responses.

Tools for active listening include employing pauses, echoing back what has been said, making open-ended requests for more information, and offering reflections and summary statements. Listening = yes. Problem-solving for the other person = no.

Here are some suggested useful phrases and questions to use when helping someone who feels stuck. Feel free to use these like Mad Libs and make them your own.

Would you like to talk?

It sounds like this is harder than you expected.

When you've navigated something like this before, what worked well for you?

What is the hardest part?

Who in your network is supportive?

This is a difficult situation.

What would be soothing for you right now?

Where are you now? Who are you with?

If you could wave a magic wand and change one thing, what would it be?

How is this going for you right now?

How can I best help you?

This is not easy.

These practices and tools can also be applied to our own black-and-white thinking and our own stuckness. Enlisting a close friend to help with the process can be useful. I apply the brainstorming on sticky notes options to my own life whenever I feel stuck.

Tunnel vision is not a place from which to make a choice. The free-dom of movement between a variety of options allows us to be an actor in the choosing and thereby the outcome.

Identify an area in your life where you feel stuck and focused on an either/or decision. How might you apply the technique of expanding tunnel vision to stuck areas of your own life?

• What wild and outlandish options are you willing to write down?

• What possibility is created between the stuck and outlandish options?

- What happens when you are compassionate and generous with yourself and sit with your own black-and-white thinking to brainstorm 20 options?

5 | LEAKY CONTAINERS

*"My candle burns at both ends; It will not last the night;
But ah, my foes, and oh, my friends—It gives a lovely light!"*

—Edna St. Vincent Millay

You are overbooked. Again. It is not possible to multitask your way through this overcommitment. Something will have to give, and it is not just you. Are you upset at someone else for roping you into this predicament? Do you feel you were talked into something you did not really want to do? At a minimum, you are wondering why you agreed.

Emotional labor is not infinite. Ultimately, there is a maximum amount of emotional labor we can expend. We unwittingly lie to people, and to ourselves, when we overpromise or heroically pledge to do something we cannot actually deliver. The Compassionate Witness does not lie. As a leader, we choose to show up in a way that can be counted on.

When approaching an opportunity to show up as a Compassionate Witness, how might we set expectations for the interaction or relationship? Think about this part of the process as an opportunity for truth telling. To manage expectations on both sides of the encounter, define the container or medium of the relationship. Think of this as the structure for how you engage in the sweet spot—the zone of maximum opportunity. Use containers to help you define and be clear about when, where, and how you expend emotional labor. There are different types of emotional labor for different scenarios.

As a more concrete way to think about this container metaphor, imagine the wide variety of containers used for serving food: compostable, breakable, mass produced, carefully handcrafted by an artist, meant for a buffet, best used at a picnic, designed for a child's birthday party, perfect for a wedding reception. Different containers for different purposes. Just as different food containers are used depending on the occasion, we can (and should) use different boundaries—our Compassionate Witness containers—depending on the current situation.

When crafting a container, the wise leader considers: Who is this for? What is this for?

As we answer these questions for a specific situation, we must remember this is not about ourselves nor about an attachment to an outcome.

Having showed up for someone with one particular container in the past does not mean we always show up in this way. We redefine our availability through what is best for the current situation, taking into consideration our own current state of well-being and ability to deliver on promises.

Of course, there are certain people in our lives to whom we've committed large and permanent containers: our family of origin, partner, children, chosen family, best friends, and key staff members or work colleagues. In time, we might evaluate these containers to see if they continue to serve us.

For example, as our kids grow from teenagers to young adults, though our love stays the same, our boundaries and the containers for how we respond to and support them will certainly change. This is a normal, healthy part of the evolution of life and the individuation of young adults. Likewise with a mentoring relationship, as the mentee grows, the mentor removes fewer obstacles for them and supports them in taking greater risks, all of which requires recrafting the container.

In family, partner, and close friend relationships, we might re-evaluate the containers we crafted if the give and take in the relationship is no longer balanced, there is a betrayal, or either party's needs change. For instance, as our parents age, our containers for how we care for them are likely to shapeshift with their needs. While consistency and keeping our commitments is key, it is also expected and normal to re-evaluate how we choose to engage over time.

There is no need to engage in "container competition" with ourselves or anyone else. This is misspent energy that would be better directed to a thoughtful consideration of the opportunity at hand. What works for you at one point in life may or may not work at another time. Likewise for our family members, friends, colleagues, and neighbors. Judgment, toward ourselves or others, does not play a role in the Compassionate Witness journey.

Here are a few factors to consider when deciding how to create the container as we assess an opportunity to engage. With practice, these aspects can become a type of formula for determining how best to show up.

Consider mediums. Think through the mediums by which you are available. Is this an in-person-only exchange? Are you available by rapid response through text? Or follow-up through email? Is this a confidential medium? Is social media part of the medium? If we meet in person, is the place at home, the office, a coffee shop, a park, or the gym? How are these meetings or calls arranged?

Consider time. When are you available? For how long? On what days of the week? At which times of day? Over what period? Is this a crisis situation where you are available 24/7? What does the time commitment look like? Look at your calendar to know what actual time you have to commit. Knowing yourself and your availability is part of being able to tell the truth as you shape the container.

Consider the topic. While being a content expert is not required for showing up as a Compassionate Witness, understanding how certain topics trigger us or are outside our comfort zone is key to crafting a container. Be mindful of the role vicarious trauma plays in your own life. Think through your own self-disclosure. What parts of yourself do you share? Why? In the Enmeshed role, we tend to overshare ourselves—both our wounded, tragic parts and also the energy we need to sustain our own family, work, and schedule. Outsourcing for content expertise is a beautiful way to create a container and set expectations.

Consider resources. While remembering that our greatest offering is witnessing through our presence, there may also be opportunities or requests for additional resources. Are you offering time, links to materials, financial support, favors or referrals in your network, a room in your home, or time off of work? In the work setting, what resources are available through benefits or human resources? In the community, what agencies or hotlines are available?

Understanding our own current well-being as well as the exist-

NOTE TO SELF

Be
generous.
Be
truthful.

ing commitments we have made to expend emotional labor is important when assessing what bandwidth we have left to take on a new commitment. Or more accurately, what form this commitment can take. Make your container—your offering—sustainable. Once the container for a scenario or interaction is defined, hold that space precious like a baby.

To support you in crafting containers, I've created a handy guide on pages 142-143. Additional guides can be downloaded from ShowUpHard.com. I strongly suggest practicing making containers by filling out a guide for each new situation you encounter. Until your container-building muscle is strengthened and muscle memory has been instilled, help yourself to Show Up Hard by taking the time to plan. What is simultaneously generous and sustainable is your greatest offering. Do the pre-work so you are prepared when a situation arrives.

As you assess the resources you have available, survey your resource landscape and take notes in the guide on pages 144-145. What personal, work-based, community-based, and private pay resources are available?

Over time, you'll become agile and able to craft and redesign containers and make up-to-the-minute assessments of your personal resources on the fly. Sometimes as I create a container for a new situation, I imagine myself as an animated ninja from a movie—able to scale walls and jump from building to building, looking at the situation and available resources from every angle. The agility of a boundary ninja feels swift and powerful in my effort to help another.

As we create a container for each scenario, we will gain clarity on what we can and cannot give in each situation. It's not selfish to identify all the ways we are not available or not choosing to show up. In fact, the opposite is true—knowing what you choose not to do can illuminate the possibilities of what you can do. This is a place of freedom where your sustainable generosity can flow. If you feel stuck getting started with creating a container, start with the smallest container possible and expand later if needed or if possible.

CREATING A CONTAINER

MEDIUMS

Where are you available?
(in person, email, coffee shop, social media, park, home, etc.)

TOPICS

Are there off-limits topics? Triggering scenarios you will avoid?
Legal or ethical considerations?

TIME

When and for how long are you available?
(24/7, by apoinment, one time, weekly, days, or years)

RESOURCES

What personal, community-based, or work-based resources can
be offered?

RESOURCE SURVEY

PERSONAL

(Food, money, shelter, clothes, specific skills)

COMMUNITY-BASED

(Crisis lines, police non-emergency number, legal aid, teen and youth centers, low-cost or sliding-scale wellness resources: acupuncture, yoga, therapy)

WORK-BASED

(Formal or informal support including flexible time; personal, sick, family or bereavement leave; medical insurance, disability insurance, counseling, books or training, referrals)

PRIVATE PAY

(Trusted referral sources for therapy, legal support, wellness and healing resources)

Let's take a closer look at the process of creating a container with a recent near Missed Connection in my life.

Recently, I was at the corner grocery store standing in a crowded line. The woman in front of me was shifting on her feet and moving her body, unable to stand still. She kept circling too close to me and bumped into me a few times. I was annoyed. I was checking my phone every few minutes, anxious to return to work. My mind was going a mile a minute. I was not present or aware. Just annoyed. Her phone rang. She was standing so close, I overheard her clearly say, "Today is a really bad day. My sleeping bag was stolen. I've been sleeping in front of the train station. I tried to get into the shelter last night, but it was full."

My immediate response was to retreat. The story was too awful; it felt like too much for me to engage. What could I do? I am one person. I am so very busy. I told myself a story about how I am busy with work that helps others. It's okay to let this one pass. It's too big of a lift to try to do anything.

I noticed her story reminded me of my previous involvement with a local houseless man named James, with whom I'd been very engaged. This trigger or reminder sent me down a path toward not wanting to engage. (I took to using the word "houseless" because James told me he had a home: It was under the bridge, and all his things where there. He just did not, yet, have a house.)

James spent hours each day reading books on the front porch of my home, thanking me when I changed out the lightbulb to a higher wattage. I cooked his eggs when his camp stove was stolen. James knew my kids by name and kept track of their comings and goings, letting me know when I arrived home after work who was already home. Once when one of my kids got mad and ran away,

James told me which direction he went. "Give him a few minutes. He'll be back. It's not easy being his age," James advised. He talked with my kids and their friends about the local baseball team and asked about their school work. He bought candy on Halloween when we ran out and I began giving pencils away. "No one wants a pencil for trick-or-treating," he chided.

There were also neighbor complaints about my "supporting his lifestyle" and requests from local shop owners to intervene when there were issues with James's behavior. There were two visits to my home from the police regarding James. When James was suffering, our conversations could get long, and it was challenging for me to disengage as he was literally at the front of my home. Sometimes it felt like I had another child. We missed him the two times he went to rehabilitation. When his name came to the top of the city's list for a room as part of its housing program, he came to tell us goodbye, promising he'd still come back to visit. It was strange without James around.

After he left, I eyed the new houseless people who came to the neighborhood with a bit of trepidation. I don't regret our involvement with James, but I was not ready to dive in like that again. Following the "give what you have" mantra of my childhood, I'd generously and thoughtfully built a container for my relationship with James. I gave what I had: A front porch, occasional extra food (without onions—he was violently allergic), lots of conversations sprinkled with coaching, but most importantly attempting to approach him as I would any of my other neighbors, disregarding his housing status. To be clear, the giving went both ways. James kept an eye on our family and gave occasional advice to the kids. He kept me up to date on good books to read, sometimes sharing a copy of one he thought I'd like, and made sure I understood the value of taking the kids to a baseball game in the ballpark.

After James left, I failed to pause to imagine another way of engaging with my other neighbors who did not have houses. I just created a wall—Missed Connections all around.

Let's look at the container James and I created for our relationship. Various aspects of the container were explored or redefined over time, with James generally respectful of my boundaries.

Medium | In person only. Often on the front porch of my home or in our parking lot. Sometimes on the sidewalk out and about in our neighborhood. Though he sometimes had a phone, we never exchanged numbers. Our conversations were generally spontaneous, though he would wait for me if he needed to talk, and I would go looking for him if I did. We never went into each other's homes. After years of knowing him and hearing many stories about his home (about the different people he let sleep there, a fire in his home, all his belongings being stolen from him, an eviction threat from the city in an attempt to clear the property), I will admit that I was immensely curious and thought many times about asking if I could visit. Each time I would conclude such a request served me and my curiosity and was not of service to James or to our relationship.

Time | Our relationship was limited to in-person moments when we saw each other. Occasionally, he rang the doorbell when he had an urgent question or had information he thought we should know about (usually about a baseball game or his plans to be away). The relationship lasted for five or so years, for the entire time we were neighbors.

Topic | We talked about many things: recovery, managing life, the politics of the neighborhood, baseball, our family lives, James's life growing up. Off-limits topics included my becoming involved with James's interactions with the justice and public health systems.

Resources | The front porch, with a no-smoking rule strictly enforced. My presence. A posture of engaging with him like I engage with any other neighbor. Occasional leftover food, a few pans, a friend's camp stove, a blanket.

The woman in front of me at the grocery store made it to the front of the line and waved me ahead to the register as she was still on her phone. As I was being checked out by the cashier, I began to recognize my trigger, what her story reminded me of—and I challenged myself: What's the smallest container I can create to avoid a Missed Connection here? Knowing what I would not give—engaging as I had with James—freed me to lean in to what was possible in this moment. As the woman began to check out at an adjacent register, I saw her scrambling with coins to pay the total. I began crafting a container from my place of enoughness, without fear or needs of my own.

Medium | It is in person, right now.

Time | It concludes before we leave the grocery store.

Topic | I choose not to engage around any of the topics I overheard. I aim to make a contribution to the present moment.

Resources | To look her in the eye and make human connection with openness, with warm regard, and without expectation. Whatever cash is in my wallet.

I walked over to the register where she stood. I paid her bill with cash so there would be no lingering from paying with a credit card. We made eye contact and for a few seconds we held each other's gaze. I left the store as she finished checking out. It's not much. It's not actually a gesture worth mentioning, in fact. But the process is worth mentioning. For me, this small act was so much better than doing nothing at all. In the end, the gift of the interaction was for me to become more fully present in the moment.

I also know firsthand the experience of being compassionately witnessed by another and how this act of being witnessed facilitated part of my healing journey. Let's note the container created by my manager and how this held me in a time of crisis.

About six years ago, I received an unexpected phone call from my sister. My 36-year-old brother had been found dead, by suicide.

Nothing in life prepares you for this kind of loss.

I was in a stage of life of muscling through it all—in the midst of a series of crises I had learned to ride like a stoked surfer. I went to work the Monday following my brother's death after sending an email to my supervisors and close colleagues about what happened and explaining, "I don't think this will affect me much. I do no not plan on taking off work."

I needed my allocated days off for my kids' sick days and for the random days school is not in session. Going to work even when I was sick myself or dealing with major issues was part of the math that barely added up to making it through the school year.

Hazel Georgetti, my kind and wise supervisor, kept close tabs on me in the days following my brother's death. I shared with her a few of the poignantly raw parts of my grief, the edges near the devastation of my heart. I talked with her about my profound guilt and the heaviness my brother's story carried for me. Hazel responded with warmth and grace, even as I kept working. In the first moment I admitted to being in a fog and unable to think clearly, she said, "This is when you leave work. This is when you get a plane ticket and go to the funeral. You come back to us when you are ready."

Hazel made sure I had a safe way to get home and arranged for someone to check in on me later. She made sure I knew about our organization's bereavement days (and told me if I needed more time, to just talk with her), the counseling offered through human resources, and her willingness to connect me with community resources.

After I returned to work following my brother's funeral, there was a card on my desk. The card was signed front, back, and sideways in so much detail by all my co-workers. As I held the card in my hands, I realized Hazel had done what I was unable to do: communicate to my co-workers the devastating heartbreak of my loss. In an act of generosity, Hazel did the emotional labor of connecting with my colleagues on my behalf when I could not. My co-workers had written such personal notes that I knew Hazel had shared with them my story and my brother's story.

Every time I think of my brother's death, I also think of Hazel. The compassion of my supervisor allowed me to process my grief.

Hazel is now retired and I have moved on to another program within the organization. When my parents came to town a few years later, she drove from another city to meet them and to talk about their son and his death. She held my mom's hand while she cried.

This is compassion at work. This is compassion in work.

Take a moment to consider the containers described in my stories about James, the grocery store encounter, and my supervisor Hazel.

- What parts of the containers resonate for you?

- What parts of the containers did not resonate for you?

- In each of the stories, how did the container help support a sustainable response?

- How did the container support the Compassionate Witness's ability to Show Up Hard?

- What ease came because the structure of the container was in place? Ease for the giver? Ease for the receiver?

- How might you refine your practice of building containers?

Sometimes it is easier to see how containers can be thoughtfully created when we look at a situation that does not directly impact us. Take the following scenarios adapted from struggles leaders have shared with me, and use the "Creating a Container" worksheet to draft containers for the person in the helper position.

• In a one-to-one meeting with a new outreach worker, he tells me about his growing anxiety and that he is having trouble sleeping at night. He is worried about giving clients bad advice or not being able to provide the support he feels they need.

• My default is to go too far with people. I can empathize with a person with a chronic illness and want to help him return to work by hiring him. But I'm also worried about the overall health of our team, as we are a small program and other staff have been covering too much for too long.

• A member of our finance team is from a conservative background. Upon learning her co-worker's child is going through a gender transition, she asks for resources on how she might show up for her co-worker's experience when the situation violates the teachings of her church. She wants to engage but worries doing so might become too much and threaten her standing at church or become awkward with her husband, who plays a leadership role in the church.

• "I see so many people burning out," shares the leader of a community-organizing effort. "It's just been too much for too long. There seems to be no relief in sight. How can we engage in the work that matters most and sustain ourselves for the long haul?"

NOTE TO SELF

you are
a giver.

6 | VICARIOUS TRAUMA

"Trauma isn't what happens to you, it's what happens inside you."

—Gabor Maté

As my first job after graduate school, I developed a court-based domestic violence program in rural Louisiana. Day after day of stories from women of all ages and backgrounds began to fill first my brain and then my body. These stories stayed with me overnight and on the weekend, impacting how I interacted with the world. In a culture that pervasively and subtly supports violence against women, I was triggered often and without notice. Sitting in church. Hearing a joke at a dinner party. Listening to a song on the radio. Someone close to me suggested I had lost my sense of humor. I replied I didn't think there was much in this world to laugh about. I still carry the stories of these women inside me, twenty-five years later.

A few years later, a graduate student I supervised was kidnapped, raped, and murdered. She was last seen leaving our first citywide conference on violence against women. A painful irony. We'd worked together in the district attorney's office—the same place that would now prosecute the man accused of killing her. Now, going to work had many layers of meaning. While my commitment to women only grew deeper and gave me a singular cause to get out of bed each day, I struggled immensely with staying focused in the office and feeling connected to people in my personal life.

A mentor-turned-friend became my lifeline during the years it took to integrate these experiences, which required equal parts maturing and healing. A co-worker also bridged these worlds with me. The mornings that he and I walked my dogs before work were the moments I felt the most sane and alive.

Trauma is defined as a highly stressful event: A real or perceived threat to life, body, safety, sanity. This includes abuse, violence, betrayal, and situations that conjure feelings of helplessness, victimization, or loss. Examples of trauma include war, sexual assault, abuse as a child, and imbalanced power dynamics at work. Race, gender, class, immigration status, and sexual orientation all impact how traumatic day-to-day life can feel. It's important to remember the experience of trauma is in the eye of the beholder—a real or perceived threat to their life, body, safety, sanity.

The term "vicarious trauma" refers to the secondhand effects of trauma experienced by friends, family members, and helpers of the person who had a traumatic experience. Experiencing vicarious trauma is also a possibility for empaths as they consume a constant barrage of news and social media coupled with the state of chronic mild stress that the majority of adults experience. Vicarious trauma is real, and those who head out on empathy adventures with wide open hearts are vulnerable to it.

Knowing the body's innate desire to return to a state of equilibrium, you can imagine how a traumatic experience triggers our coping responses and leaves its mark in the narrative of our life story.

Comparing one trauma to another, scaling them, does not serve you on your journey as an empathetic leader. A traumatic response is a traumatic response. Our healing is a journey. Judgment in the process will not serve you or the other in creating needed change.

~~what's~~
~~wrong?~~
what
happened?

Likewise with vicarious trauma. The days I berated myself for my lack of focus at work and struggle to intimately connect amounted to misspent energy. This was all part of the internal dialogue directed by survivor's guilt. I had important work to do for myself. Diminishing my own mental fog in comparison with someone else's fractured or lost life meant I did not allow space to tenderly care for my own broken heart. Comparing serves neither.

As we embark on our empathy adventures, stay curious as to whether a sticky story or a triggering situation may have a traumatic experience behind it. This is true for both our own sticky stories and triggers as well as the sticky stories and triggers of those around us.

Consider this: Those we refer to as "difficult people" are often not difficult by personality, but, rather, are people who have experienced difficulty in life and have been unable to integrate the trauma. Or they may be people who have experienced difficulty and are not best served by their current life situation. Separating the "difficult" from the person and instead making it part of the experience may help us to find a path forward as we seek to make change.

Depending on where we lead and where we are creating change, becoming trauma aware and trauma informed may be a beneficial, and in fact often necessary, part of the change-making we seek. Small changes in work culture norms can have an enormous impact on how we are able to bring our whole selves to work. What happens when self-care is a celebrated part of the work culture rather than overgiving being the crowning achievement? What shifts when we ground the beginning and end of our workdays with ritual?

My co-worker Karishma Oza has implemented a ritual during our clinic's weekly meetings when we discuss each patient. We now begin each of these case conferences with a brief check-in, taking turns naming aloud a high and a low from the last week. No commentary or fixing required. Just the opportunity to speak a piece of truth from our own lives before we go about the important and profound work of serving others.

In order to engage with empathy, we must be aware of the traumas that are part of many people's lived experience. As a leader who chooses to Show Up Hard and as we engage as a Compassionate Witness with others, there is the necessary overlap with others' traumas and the potential for transfer to occur. To sustain ourselves as we lead with empathy, we commit to also seeing and noticing the lifelong impact trauma has on our own life and ability to cope. Noticing and acknowledging vicarious trauma is an act of generosity.

I carry inside me the stories of hundreds of traumas. I would not have it any other way. This is part of how I Show Up Hard in the world. While I will never forget these stories, they are no longer shouting inside my head and aching in my bones. These stories inform how I view the world and the choices I make. The balance for me lies in the integration of rituals at work and at home alongside powerful, intimate relationships.

Taking good care is the hallmark of the Compassionate Witness.

NOTE TO SELF

take
good
care.

BOOK THREE

Arriving

You are not a drop in the ocean. You are the entire ocean in a drop.

—Rumi

You've learned the framework and skills. You've traversed the detours. You've arrived. Wecome! This is not the end. It is actually the beginning. You will forever journey forward with the know-how to sustain yourself on the Show Up Hard path.

11 | THE INTERSECTION OF EMPATHY AND RESILIENCE

"The plain fact is that the world does not need more successful people, but it does desperately need more peacemakers, healers, restorers, storytellers, and lovers of every kind. It needs people who live well in their places. It needs people of moral courage willing to join the fight to make the world habitable and humane."

—David Orr

Nearing the end of yoga class, we came to a seated position on our mats and began the integration of learnings from class. Crystal Higgins, our brilliant teacher, gently coached, "Strong back. Soft front." While Crystal was referring to the poses we had done for our backs, along with the positions to open our hearts, I immediately thought about meeting you here. At the intersection of empathy and resilience. We are here with strong backs and soft fronts— ready with the framework to hold our wild and open hearts on the Show Up Hard path.

The intersection of empathy and resilience is yours. Own it.

We've learned heaps of skills and had some sneak peeks at a few scary detours. And yet, you are here.

This mash-up of empathy and resilience is your productive place. Your ability to notice and to observe the space between us provides your perspective. This is the place from which you will make the most change. Where you will be the most yourself.

Where empathy and resilience meet is one of my favorite places to hangout. Being at this intersection has come to have that familiar calm feeling of returning home.

Create comfort with this location. An ease. Find the many paths leading back here so you can come here often.

Strong back, soft front—you are ready.

The feeling you were born for this moment? Believe it.

2 | AUTOMATE RESILIENCY

"Go back and take care of yourself. Your body needs you, your feelings need you, your perceptions need you. Your suffering needs you to acknowledge it. Go home and be there for all these things."

—Thich Nhat Hanh

After learning to put myself on the to-do list, I became increasingly aware of myself and my giving as I showed up for others. The practice of calendaring wellness activities provided a visual for keeping myself and my boundaries as part of the planning process for my week. Beyond this basic awareness, which allows us to craft the circles framework and engage with others, we need to deepen our commitment to our own resilience and automate those investments to sustain ourselves for our empathy adventures.

A basic tenet of financial counseling is to implement a savings plan. Even if you are paying off debt, a wise financial counselor will advise you to set up an automatic and regular savings plan. Perhaps this is five dollars from each paycheck or a certain percentage of your take-home pay. The goal is to make savings a practice. By automating the practice, we make it easy to adhere to the savings plan. Investing in the future has literal and figurative gains.

Likewise, you will gain by automating investments in your resiliency.

You may avoid resilience investments, believing you don't have the time or money. A resilience practice can begin wherever you are now and expanded in time as your Show Up Hard practice develops. Neither time nor money is required to pay homage to resilience. Intention is the key.

My deepest resilience practices developed during a period of life when I rarely had time to myself and little disposable income. When I first divorced, my kids qualified for reduced-price breakfast and lunch at school. I could not afford all the aftercare we needed, trading teaching cooking classes at their after-school program for the childcare fees I was unable to pay. I knew I had to create ways to put on my own oxygen mask so I would have the stamina to take care of my kids for the long haul. I learned the best self-care practices are free.

The constraints of time and money brought myriad magical ways I found to refresh. Part of the trick was reminding myself of the truth: "This is a great break!" or "This is a treat!" Dancing in the kitchen—with or without the kids. Night hikes and treasure hunts in the canyon near our home to experience nature. Taking classes at the public library and recreation center. Making large batches of food and trading with a friend for a night off of cooking. Hula-hooping in the hallway when there wasn't time for a run. Making art out of found wood and paint. Enjoying a cup of tea while looking out the window. Camping with friends. Anything by candlelight.

Don't get me wrong—I love a massage. A long run. My gym membership. Dance class. Travel. But I'm immensely grateful for the period in my life that taught me the true magic of intention as a form of resilience. I associate an abundance of delight with those also challenging years. Awe and devotion became a part of my intentional path, the strength behind my will to Show Up Hard every day. The intention we bring to our daily activities, our attention, and the stories we tell ourselves are all part of investing in resilience. Ritual reminds us. Ritual can become the trigger for resetting our thoughts, our breath, our course of action. As the monk and peace activist Thich Nhat Hanh teaches us, with intention, washing the dishes can become a prayer.

When you consider your resiliency investment needs, covering the basics is a great place to start. How much and at what time is the right sleep for your body? How much and what foods nourish you? What exercise needs do you have? For a vibrant resiliency plan, consider your personal needs for a mindfulness, spiritual, or ritual practice; creative projects; and other practices that bring you to your place of enoughness. A thriving practice of investing in our own resiliency supports us in operating from our place of enoughness. Only you will know what it takes to sustain you so you can operate from a place of truthful generosity.

Understanding our personal baseline requirements to maintain a sense of wholeness and stability helps to illuminate what additional self-care will be needed if we find ourselves in a crisis, depleted, or resentful. These booster self-care practices can also be timed on a monthly, quarterly, or yearly basis as an investment to keep our practice of giving and receiving in alignment. At the first sign of our own crisis state or burn out, at the top of the to-do list will be developing a plan for our self-care activities.

This resiliency investment not only supports us as we keep the Enmeshed role at bay, but also allows us to be grounded enough to avoid a Missed Connection response. One manager once shared with me during a workshop: "In order for my mind and body to be connected—to be present and empathetic for others—I have to go to the gym each morning to get grounded in my body. Without that routine, I'm really challenged to be there for others. This practice has changed my relationship and emotional availability for my partner and kids, as well. My family actively supports me in getting to the gym each morning before work."

Resilience is a journey, not a destination. In our fast-paced world where so much competes for our attention, a wise leader recognizes sustaining oneself is not a luxury but a key to thriving. A resiliency plan is best incorporated as a habit, a ritual—part of your commitment to showing up as a Compassionate Witness.

In the fall of 2017 as the #MeToo movement grew, I found myself in a vortex of phone calls, text messages, and email exchanges with women as we supported each other in a number of ways: holding institutions accountable, lifting up women who publicly came forward with stories, and supporting teams and co-workers triggered by the repeated and violent news. One of my absolute Show Up Hard venues is for women speaking out against and healing from sexual and physical trauma. Tarana Burke, founder of the #MeToo movement, said during her plenary talk at the Wisdom 2.0 conference in 2018, "Am I going to be in conflict or am I going to be of service?" This is a philosophy that resonates deeply with me. Being of service in the era of #MeToo is powerful work for a Compassionate Witness.

Early one morning, I received a text: "Can you talk right now?" Both by the time of day and the tenor of the text, I knew to drop everything and call this colleague. She answered the phone with a shaky voice, and I knew in my bones what was coming next. I stood up and looked out the window so I would be present for her words. I became observant of my breathing, hoping to mirror for her calmness and presence as she spoke and I listened from a distance. I consciously widened my shoulders and opened my chest, a posture of openness I would have taken if we were in person. I wanted her to know through the cellular telephone connection: I'm here, I am receiving your story.

"I believe you," I said. "I want you to know this is not your fault." We talked further, and I offered the help that fit the container I had available for the day. My offering was both generous and sustainable.

When I hung up the phone, I reoriented myself to what remained of the day. I made sure I had plans to attend my regularly scheduled dance class that night. At dinner with my family after dance class, I was quieter than usual. "While I can't share details," I said, "I want you to know I listened to a #MeToo story today and I'm exceptionally sad and tired. I'm going to bed early and am going on a run in the morning. I'm okay, but I'm quiet so I can take it all in and restore myself."

I needed to check my ego more than a few times to be sure my engagement was not around a narrative of "saving" someone. I had to remind myself a few times about the container I had chosen. Even after decades of practice, this is still a journey for me—a journey that works, yet one that is also active and dynamic. This journey to Show Up Hard grows stronger and stronger the more I do it.

Whenever you encounter a personal crisis or an opportunity to show up as a Compassionate Witness for another, increase your attention to your own resiliency practice. Each act of investing in our own resiliency becomes a sign of our willingness to Show Up Hard for others.

Using the "Resiliency Landscape" worksheet, jot down resilience practices that sustain you on the fly, on the regular, and in crisis.

ON THE FLY, WHEN NEEDED

What are quick and easy resiliency investments?
(Mindful-breathing, looking out the window, taking a break, listening to music)

MONTHLY/QUARTERLY

What are less frequent but available resiliency investments?
(Vacation, staycation, retreat, offline time)

WEEKLY

What are scheduled and regular resiliency investments?
(Exercise, journal, meditation, spiritual practice)

IN CRISIS

When things fall apart, what basics are required?
(Types of food, sleep patterns, centering practices)

3 | COMMIT TO POSSIBILITY

"I imagine that yes is the only living thing."

—E. E. Cummings

"A flower does not think of competing with the flower next to it. It just blooms."

—Sensei Ogui

A client might ask, "If you were in my situation, what would you do?" We may ask ourselves when in a state of disequilibrium for similar advice from a trusted friend or colleague. Yet who goes to sleep with this decision? Who wakes up with the consequences— for better or worse—of the decision? Do we ever, in the end, know what is best for someone else?

As we practice showing up as a Compassionate Witness, we can level up by a continued non-attachment to outcome and an openness to possibility. It's human to seek the comfort that comes with a sense of knowing where we are going. It can feel easier to embark if we have a checklist or an algorithm. Will you systematize my Compassionate Witness journey, pretty please?! In reality, our attachment to outcome stifles possibility.

At social work school, we learn to be unattached to the outcome in relation to client autonomy and self-determination. Putting aside our own biases, beliefs, and goals for what success looks like is key to supporting people on their own paths. As such, there are not prescribed formulas or algorithms for finding solutions. There are theories. There are frameworks to provide structure. There are screening tools. There are support systems. Yet the outcome belongs solely to the client. That said, when you work long enough with a certain topic, you begin to see patterns emerge. Without paying diligent attention to non-attachment, you might find yourself putting people in boxes based on their stories or your first impressions.

The power of Showing Up Hard is not dependent on seeing the situation through to the end nor is it dependent on knowing the outcome. My career is filled with programs based on the principles of brief intervention: a crisis hotline, a hotline for HIV providers, referrals for HIV-affected couples who want to conceive, an online chat service linking to HIV prevention resources. In all these settings, it has been challenging to define success by the outcome of where a person ends up days, weeks, or years down the road. It's the evaluation struggle of my career. Sure, sometimes I get the thrill of a birth announcement, or bump into a provider at a conference who tells the story of a successful patient outcome, or hear back from one of the chat visitors that the referral was a success. However, each of the services we provide is self-elected, without a requirement for follow up, and often the interaction is anonymous, though the caller or visitor is always welcome to return. This constraint, though, allows for a focus and precision on the present—on how we engage. We gauge our success on the quality of our work in the moment: our openness, our searching for the question behind the question, and our modeling of warm regard.

Historian and religious scholar James Carse describes a different framework related to a posture of non-attachment to outcomes in the book *Finite and Infinite Games*. Carse explores the grand possibilities that arise when we choose to explore a way of living outside the traditional win-or-lose paradigm. What happens when you reimagine a game (or life) as not having an end (or solution), but rather as a set of moves (decisions) where each move impacts yet another opportunity to play?

In Buddhism, pure in-the-moment presence and non-attachment are believed to be an enlightened status, a higher way of being.

Regardless of what theory personally brings you comfort, finding yourself steady in the face of the unknown can yield opportunities beyond your expectations.

The following story is a powerful lesson illustrating the vastness of possibility.

My desk was in the dim hallway of Louisiana's St. Charles Parish Courthouse, behind a gated wall and locked door. At this desk, I helped people file restraining orders and supported people through criminal cases of domestic violence. To get to my desk, all visitors had to be screened by the sheriff's department and pass-through a metal detector. The deputy on duty would call me when someone arrived for an appointment so I could meet them at the sheriff's station, just after the metal detectors, and walk them to my semiprivate desk.

One day my phone rang, with the security deputy on the other end of the line: "A lady is here who refuses to sign in or give her name, says she has an appointment with you. She is carrying a huge purse that she does not want to let go of." In our first meeting, Charlotte had little to say. When I asked, "How do you think I can be helpful?," she matter-of-factly replied, "I don't know." I talked about a few of the ways I could help people, attempting to normalize the topics of intimate partner violence and getting help. Upon hearing about the afternoon support group at the social service agency next door, Charlotte asked if I would write that information down so she could give it to her neighbor. I learned Charlotte does not drive. The neighbor who brought her also took her to other appointments for her eight-year-old son. Charlotte appeared to be in her early 50s and had a 27-year-old daughter from a previous marriage who lived a few parishes away. The entire conversation was devoid of emotion and entirely unremarkable, except for the very large purse she kept clutched on her lap.

Charlotte attended the next support group. Support group occurred at the same time as school pickup, so Charlotte was not missed from the day's routine, as everyone, including her husband, believed she was in the car with the neighbor for carpool. Every Monday, Charlotte attended support group. She sat in the same chair. She said very little. She kept an obsessive watch on her large purse, which she tucked under her chair with a strap looped around her ankle.

Over the weeks of seeing her in group, and occasional individual visits to me at the courthouse (always dropped off by the neighbor, and always with a story so she would not be missed from the daily routine), I began to notice that Charlotte only took the most necessary of information on paper and always gave it to her neighbor. Charlotte had a calm demeanor, yet refused to sign in with the sheriff's department and was adamant that she not let go of her purse.

In time, I learned the purse held all her important documents and papers related to two large settlement checks she said would soon come in the mail. She kept the papers with her so she would be ready when the checks arrived. She had committed to memory the details of her case, including exact dates, over the many years it had been ongoing, would quote bits of correspondence, and could repeat the full names of various people who had worked on the case. The details came in a long rambling story she told in detail and frequently. To be truthful, I never believed the checks were coming. It seemed like magical thinking and a way to avoid dealing with her current life. Except, she did deal with her current life. She came to support group. She made plans to minimize the violence at home. She recognized her son was impacted by the abuse and followed up on referrals. She listened intently to the stories of other women in support group as they detailed plans to leave their partners as well as when they reconciled.

If I had been attached to the outcome of Charlotte's story, I would have predicted she would never leave her partner and success would have looked like supporting her when she became suicidal, which she occasionally did, and helping her continue to create safety and well-being for her son.

Unattached to the outcome, this is what happened.

The week of Thanksgiving is notoriously slow at the courthouse. Dockets are cleared. Skeleton crews staff the building. I worked Monday through Wednesday and expected to be bored. On Monday afternoon, during carpool time, my desk phone rang. "The lady with the purse is here," the deputy said. I met Charlotte and we walked to my desk. She sat down, purse on her lap, and said, "The checks arrived today. I'm ready." Surprised, I asked, "Ready for what?"

"I'm ready to leave," she said. "You told me when I was ready to leave, you'd help me. I have the checks. I'm leaving and I'm taking my son."

She took out the checks, and sure enough, they offered two large chunks of money that would easily cover living expenses for many months, perhaps a year. I learned she had never had a bank account and did not know how to cash or write checks.

Her plan: She had made arrangements, using her neighbor's telephone, to rent a small apartment above a laundromat near one of the few bus stops in town. The apartment came with a stove and refrigerator and she planned to do laundry downstairs. Since she would no longer be close to the helpful neighbor, she planned to take her son to school on the bus. Her new landlord was holding the apartment and she needed to bring him a check the next day. Her husband planned to spend Thanksgiving with his adult children from a previous marriage in a nearby town and was not expected home until evening. She and her son had permission to stay home. After her husband left on Thanksgiving morning, she had arranged for her neighbor's husband to pull up with a U-Haul truck. Each week for several years, when she brought home groceries, she would stash an item or two in the attic in boxes labeled with her older daughter's name, slowly replacing her daughter's belongings with the pantry items for the new home she dreamed of having. For the first time in the many months I'd known her, she cracked a small smile. "We could live for months on just what I have in the attic." She was proud of herself. I could see why.

I grabbed my checkbook and taught her how to write checks and use the transaction register. We walked across the street to the bank to open a checking account. When the bank teller listed all the documents needed to open the account, my heart sank, as there was not time to get everything together and Charlotte needed her apartment deposit check the next day. As I argued for an exception to the rules, Charlotte grabbed my arm and smiled again, saying, "Oh, don't you worry. I have everything right here in my purse." She produced the myriad required documents and opened a checking account. She wrote her first check to her new landlord. On Thursday morning, Thanksgiving Day, the U-Haul backed up to her house. She packed it. They left.

That's not the end of the story.

A few weeks into the new year, she called me from the phone in her new home (a little miracle all its own, to talk with her on the phone) and declared, "I want to get a job. It needs to be a job Monday through Friday, from eight-thirty in the morning to three in the afternoon. I don't want to leave my son alone after school. He's already been through too much. Let me know if you hear of anything!" My internal response was: It was a long shot. Within a few days, she'd found a job across the street from the bus stop where she waited with her son. The store owner needed some extra hands and appreciated her desired schedule. So, after waiting at the bus stop in the morning with her son, she walked across the street to work. A few minutes before three, she returned to the bus stop to pick him up. My morning commute took me right past this bus stop. Charlotte took such delight as she subtly waved as I drove by. I liked this remaining connection, as she no longer came to support group.

Many months later, she called again: "I'd like to get a driver's license. Do you know anyone who can help me learn to drive?" I had recently given a talk at the local women's organization, whose members had been eager to help with such things. They'd donated quarters for women to make payphone calls, but many members had asked if they could do something more. I called and asked if there was someone who could teach Charlotte to drive. Imagine my smile when I saw Charlotte driving around town behind the wheel of a fancy car with the Republican Women's Club member in the passenger seat! Charlotte got her driver's license and bought an old, reliable car, which gave her the ability to drive to see her daughter.

I think of Charlotte often. Especially when my personal prospects look dim. Or when I start imagining I know the answer to someone else's problem. A little Charlotte energy goes a long way to supporting detachment from the outcome and inviting possibility.

NOTE TO SELF

Uncertainty
is actually
possibility
wearing her
winter coat.

Invite her in.
Help her with her coat.

4 | PRACTICE IS A PRACTICE

When I reflect on my journey, I'm reminded how we build skill and muscle memory to support our emotional labor and the commitment we have made to Show Up Hard as a leader in the face of uncertainty. Here are few nuggets of wisdom I rely upon often.

Permission granted | I wave my magic wand over you: permission is granted. Do not wait to be invited to the journey. No formal invitation will be issued. No promotion. No announcement. You may avoid the journey because of self-doubt or fear. We often hide from showing up to do the good work our gifts, privilege, or opportunity beg of us. Permission is granted. Go.

Begin here | No need to wait until you know all the answers or have all the skills or arrive in a new place of knowing. It's not required. Begin here. Now. Right where you are. Begin the journey.

Learn by experience | Compassion and connection are learned by experience. No doubt reading books, attending a course, or talking can help guide or inspire us. Attending a workshop can be useful. But to truly learn to give and receive compassion, to experience connection at a deep level, we have to do it. Compassion and connection are skills that can be built, like a muscle, and refined over time. Muscle memory is likewise developed as part of the process of doing. To embody compassion and connection we must do compassion and connection.

Make mistakes | Learning by doing means we'll make mistakes. It's part of the process. Just like you would coach a student to have a growth mindset about mistakes, allow yourself this same learning opportunity. Make mistakes—your know-how, skills, and emotional muscle memory will evolve in this process. And find the means to be gentle with yourself in the process.

Try again | Commit to continuing to show up, to trying again—even when you're feeling bruised or red-faced. We might feel embarrassment or disappointment via learning experiences on the journey. Be brave and try again. There is no doubt it takes guts. Courage is the badge of the Compassionate Witness.

Live out loud | Hiding will stunt the entire journey—both yours and that of those you seek to serve. How might we live out loud on this journey? Consider empathy adventures as opportunities to "stamp your passport" in the emotional world. You have permission to show up in new ways, to create containers to support change-making, and to embrace your own growth even as you are on a journey to deeply support those you seek to serve.

Do the hard work of creating definition | Defining boundaries takes concerted effort and conscious attention, and the process may be painful. Just like the bodybuilder seeks to define a specific muscle, getting the boundaries for certain situations just right takes serious attention. Moving from a Enmeshed or Missed Connection role to one of a Compassionate Witness can be like constructing a new building or town. That is to say, intimidating! Both as my children have grown and as intimate personal connections with friends have evolved, at times it has been deeply painful to craft new boundaries to best meet the needs of the new situation. But it's all progress.

Be gentle | Being gentle is always an option. Finding compassion for ourselves is a prerequisite to find and express compassion for others. Being gentle with ourselves is a great way to practice and be able to soften our posture toward others. When feeling strong emotion toward a person or a situation, pause to consider how things might shift if you are gentle with yourself. Or gentle with the person or situation. What new insights emerge?

Find travel buddies | Empathy adventures go well with likemind-ed companions. Find those who can hold both your brightest and your darkest days. Some people are scared of our brightest light. Not to worry—they may have their place in other parts of our life. Knowing who in our life can hold the truth of all that we are results in the kind of support we seek for our Compassionate Witness work.

Get unstuck | Since this is a living-out-loud process, it means we'll get stuck now and again. My newest effort to "unstuck" myself is to frankly contemplate whether I want to be right, or whether I want to create change. Remembering why I chose to show up illuminates a path forward. Even if that path is uncertain, I no longer feel stuck.

Honor confidentiality | There are zero points for bragging, gossiping, or using our Compassionate Witness experiences to posture or position ourselves. None. There is honor in holding close the precious moments of sweet-spot engagement, knowing that another would do the same for us.

Be dependable | There is power in being consistent and dependable. The opposite is also true: Being inconsistent undermines the process and your trustworthiness. A consistent person can be a powerful force. Leaders keep promises. Be mindful of what you promise, and then do it.

Be real | Be gentle with yourself. This is a lifelong journey. Consider this sage wisdom from the Skin Horse in The Velveteen Rabbit:

> "Real isn't how you are made," said the Skin Horse. "It's a thing that happens to you. When a child loves you for a long, long time, not just to play with, but REALLY loves you, then you become Real."

> "Does it hurt?" asked the Rabbit.

> "Sometimes," said the Skin Horse, for he was always truthful. "When you are Real you don't mind being hurt."

> "Does it happen all at once, like being wound up," he asked, "or bit by bit?"

> "It doesn't happen all at once," said the Skin Horse. "You become. It takes a long time. That's why it doesn't happen often to people who break easily, or have sharp edges, or who have to be carefully kept. Generally, by the time you are Real, most of your hair has been loved off, and your eyes drop out and you get loose in the joints and very shabby. But these things don't matter at all, because once you are Real you can't be ugly, except to people who don't understand."

It's a joy to meet you on this journey. May we build our empathy muscles to naturally create, invite, and allow change as we Show Up Hard through our role as a Compassionate Witness.

Dawn breaks
each morning
without
permission.

Follow her lead.

5 | RETURNING TO EQUILIBRIUM, CHANGED

"I am always at the beginning."

—The aged Buddha

Early one Saturday morning, I was in conversation with a colleague who had reached out for support. While he had developed confidence in being a Compassionate Witness at work, Showing Up Hard for others, he had been knocked off balance by a situation at home. "Why is this so hard?" he asked, his voice cracking. He had begun to question himself in his own crisis.

It's hard because you care. It's hard because the stakes are high. It's hard because it is you who *can* show up even in the face of this situation that has rocked your world. It's hard every time, I told him. The sheer magnitude is also the exquisite beauty of this journey. Yes, we build skill and hone our ability to shape containers and develop a network of supporting resources. And yet there are situations that bring us to our knees. That take our breath away. That shock us with their gravity. It is then that we return to the beginning, to the *why*.

I reminded my colleague of how he had built his Show Up Hard practice at work: Step by step. In fact, he reminded me, it was the small changes he made that led to huge outcomes for all. We mused on what that might look like now for him, at home.

We are the ones who choose to Show Up Hard, to support forward motion, to be catalysts for change. To be in relentless pursuit of the possible, we have to do the hard work of dancing with our egos, investing in our emotional labor, and making deposits in our own resiliency. We return again and again to the basics of the Show Up Hard practice. Because we can. Because it works. Because the world needs you in this moment. Right now.

As we Show Up Hard, we ourselves are changed. Through risk and reward, we arrive at a new state of equilibrium in our practice as a Compassionate Witness.

For so many of us, this work is more than a career or job—it is a way of life. We do this work because we are called. Underneath the relentless optimism and dogged determination is a fear that whatever time we have to dedicate will not be enough—we will not learn enough, give enough, make enough progress. We will miss an opportunity. To calm this nagging fear, we march and write and try again and innovate and rally. Our truest work is offering the best of whatever we have: A wicked smart brain, boundless compassion, mad organizational skills, the drive to volunteer for the late shift, a clear rallying call, bold truth-telling, skilled data analysis, or holding space with the invitation "all are welcome." We believe the collective sum of our individual efforts is far greater than the simple sum of the parts. We throw our very best in—whatever the size or scale of the offering. By individually offering the best of ourselves, we contribute to the continuous momentum of progress we believe will ultimately tip and become a downhill sprint. With this belief comes the invisible and powerful connection to all those who have made their own offerings.

The end is really the beginning. Opportunities to create change present themselves often and without notice.

Now, go Show Up Hard as only you can.

NOTE TO SELF

Begin here.

APPENDIX
RESOURCES
SUGGESTED READING

APPENDIX |
PAYING IT FORWARD

My deep wish is that *Show Up Hard* becomes more than a book for you, that it becomes a conversation starter for you with your teams and support network. The Show Up Hard framework is the rallying call for resilience as we seek to make the world a better place. I've created resources on the Show Up Hard website (www.ShowUpHard.com) to support you in incorporating this practice into your day-to-day life. The website also has videos and downloads you can share with your team.

If you enjoyed this book, you might:

- ✓ Write in the book. Tear it apart. Carry pieces with you. Make it yours.
- ✓ Share a copy with your team, co-workers, or support network.
- ✓ Use the downloadable worksheets on the website (referenced throughout the book) to guide conversations with team members or your support network.
- ✓ Share the worksheets in a book club, women's or men's circle, or leadership group to support other change-makers who are Showing Up Hard.

Material to augment your Show Up Hard adventures can be found at ShowUpHard.com, including:

- ✓ Note to Self printable and shareable files.
- ✓ A newsletter that allows you to be the first to learn about trainings, workshops, and new content.
- ✓ Worksheets and tools. Feel free to print multiple copies. Blow them up a size and stick them to the wall as a reminder or for use in a team meeting. Use a pencil, a permanent marker, or sticky notes to complete the worksheets.
- ✓ Videos on key principles and stories not included in the book.
- ✓ Suggested reading lists of additional books, articles, and videos.

You can find more of my love for you at:

www.xoShannonWeber.com
www.LoveYou2.org
www.HIVEonline.org
www.PleasePrEPMe.org
www.PleasePrEPMe.global

RESOURCES AND SUGGESTED READING

"7 Steps for Dealing with Difficult People,"
by the Chopra Center (article)
A short article to bookmark and review before a challenging
 conversation. www.chopra.com/articles/7-steps-for-dealing-
with-difficult-people

Beyond Compassion Manifesto
(downloadable and printable resource)
Postcard and poster versions of a manifesto championing
resilience and healing. www.hiveonline.org/gift-manifesto-
toward-resilience-healing

*The Body Keeps the Score: Brain, Mind, and Body in the
Healing of Trauma*
by Bessel van der Kolk, MD (book)
A quintessential primer on the research of healing trauma and
the life's work of van der Kolk.

The Center for Nonviolent Communication
(website, training, forum)
The nonviolent communication framework teaches skills for
active listening and how to engage with another. A great place
to begin for skill-building. www.cnvc.org

*The Coaching Habit: Say Less, Ask More & Change the Way
You Lead Forever*
by Michael Bungay Stanier (book)

An easy-to-read book offering a highly applicable approach to listening with a posture toward supporting another's growth.

Difficult Conversations: How to Discuss What Matters Most
by Douglas Stone, Bruce Patton, and Sheila Heen (book)
A detailed and powerful examination of how to manage challenging conversations, from the same Harvard-based group behind *Getting to Yes*.

Daring Greatly: How the Courage to Be Vulnerable Transforms the Way We Live, Love, Parent, and Lead
by Brené Brown (book)
Brown's stellar examination of the power of vulnerability, the embracing of fear, and the courage to show up.

"Empathy: The Human Connection to Patient Care"
by Cleveland Clinic (video)
A powerful four-minute video to practice the beginning of our empathy adventures, noticing our responses.
www.youtu.be/cDDWvj_q-o8

Engaging Difficult People: 100 Practical Lessons on Empathy and How It Transforms Relationships
by Laura Tyson (book)
Short, digestible chapters full of ideas and actionable changes to expand our capacity for empathy.

"Everything You Think You Know about Addiction is Wrong,"
by Johann Hari (TED Talk)
Transcendental talk concluding that the power of connection overcomes the disease of addiction. www.ted.com/talks/johann_hari_everything_you_think_you_know_about_addiction_is_wrong

Getting to Yes: Negotiating Agreements without Giving In
by Roger Fisher and William Ury (book)
A classic from the Harvard Negotiation Project that is useful for a humane and skills-based posture for approaching conflict.

How Al-Anon Works: For Family & Friends of Alcoholics (book)
The classic blue book for family and friends of those who dance with addiction. It offers a helpful framework for anyone who easily slips into an Enmeshed way of engaging and a way of life for boundary ninjas.

"In a Difficult Conversation, Listen More Than You Talk"
by Emma Seppala and Jennifer Stevenson (article)
Bookmark this gem and return to it often, particularly when you worry you won't know the right answer. Be reminded you don't need to know anything; you just need to listen. www.hbr.org/2017/02/in-a-difficult-conversation-listen-more-than-you-talk

My Grandmother's Hands: Racialized Trauma and the Pathway to Mending Our Hearts and Bodies
by Resmaa Menakem (book)
A powerful framework to inform our body-centered leadership. As a social worker, Menakem brings a systems approach to his insightful analysis and the path forward.

Nonviolent Communication: A Language of Life
by Marshall B. Rosenberg (book)
The nonviolent communication framework teaches offers skills for active listening and how to engage with another. A great place to begin for skill-building.

Recovery: Freedom from Our Addictions
by Russell Brand (book)
Brand gives a 21st-century facelift to the twelve steps and includes modern addictions like technology. Be inspired to look at patterns in your own life as well as to compassionately support those around you.

Rising Strong: How the Ability to Reset Transforms the Way We Live, Love, Parent, and Lead
by Brené Brown (book)
A how-to book for examining our sticky stories and reshaping the narrative of our lives. Brown weaves her hallmark vulnerability and courage throughout.

"Sonder: The Realization That Everyone Has a Story"
by the Dictionary of Obscure Sorrows (video)
This video is worth bookmarking and returning to regularly as a reminder. www.youtu.be/AkoML0_FiV4

"Sympathy vs. Empathy,"
by Brené Brown (video)
Three-minute animated video detailing the differences between sympathy and empathy. www.youtu.be/KZBTYViDPlQ

"Ten Keys to Handling Unreasonable & Difficult People"
by Preston Ni (article)
Tips for creating our containers to maximize forward motion when we find ourselves stewards of change with a challenging person. www.psychologytoday.com/us/blog/communication-success/ 201309/ten-keys-handling-unreasonable-difficult-people

There Is No Good Card for This: What to Say and Do When Life Is Scary, Awful, and Unfair to People You Love
by Kelsey Crowe and Emily McDowell (book)
A gorgeous and incredibly practical book for empathy basics in a wide variety of life scenarios. Excellent content for empathy skill-building.

"This Is Your Body on Stress"
by Laura Shocker (article and infographic)
Understanding the basics behind fight or flight responses is helpful for noticing our own responses. www.huffingtonpost.com/2013/03/19/body-stress-response_n_2902073.html

The Trauma of Everyday Life
by Mark Epstein, MD (book)
A Buddhist approach to growth and a way forward for the traumas we encounter on our life journeys.

Trauma Stewardship: An Everyday Guide to Caring for Self While Caring for Others
by Laura van Dernoot (book)
Van Dernoot maps a way forward for knowing our own empathy adventures and investing in resilience. The Trauma Stewardship website and forum and "Trauma Stewardship" TED Talk will be go-to resources for those in the day-to-day work of creating change in the world and lives around them.
www.traumastewardship.com

"W.A.I.T Why Am I Talking?"
by Dan Pezullo (infographic)
Gem of a map as to why you would speak in a meeting, which is also useful for examining why we talk in a variety of life settings.

www.communities.nasponline.org/blogs/dan-pezzulo/
2017/02/01/wait

Waking the Tiger: Healing Trauma
by Peter A. Levine (book)
A classic in understanding how the body processes trauma and
ways forward for healing from traumatic experiences.

When Things Fall Apart: Heart Advice for Difficult Times
by Pema Chödrön (book)
Chödrön's spiritual approach to facing life's challenges.
Easy to pick up again and again to supercharge our presence
and resilience.

"Women, HIV and Trauma: Toward Resiliency & Healing"
by Shannon Weber (article), including "beyond compassion," by
Silvi Alcivar (poem)
A poet weaves the light and dark of showing up with compassion
and championing resiliency. www.huffingtonpost.com/
shannon-weber/women-hiv-and-trauma-towa_b_10489298.html

ACKNOWLEDGMENTS

It takes a village to do much of anything worthwhile. Writing this book has been an experience of gratitude and appreciation for the connected web of wonder in which I live.

What I know about giving has been shaped by my loving parents and thirteen siblings: Ross, Michael, Kathleen, Saul, Jacob, Marieta, Ashley, Alyce, Amaris, Camilla, Tyson, Seth, and Boyce. Webers, you are a bounty of goodness and I'm so grateful to be one of you.

Dr. Elizabeth Rayne, my first social work mentor, professor, and then supervisor, with whom my social work soul was created. I feel her spirit with me whenever I face a difficult choice.

Colleagues turned friends, the ultimate guides in my Show Up Hard practice in the workplace: Patricia Wood Davis, Marciana Popescu, Melissa Heckman, Deb Cohan, Jess Waldura, Megan Huchko, and Judy Auerbach.

The writing and creation of this book has been cheered on mightily by a crew of magnificent humans who have rallied strong.

Thank you, Kelli Wood, for asking me powerful questions as only you can, and then listening to the answers. Your constant drive to create a better world inspires me.

All the heart-eyes to my mastermind group for the consistency, the bigger box, and the wisdom: Travis Allison, Peter Nieuwenhuizen, Conor McCarthy, and Laura Tyson.

Conversations and feedback from these wise ones catapulted deeper dives and nuance: altMBA alumni community, Andrea Tarrell, Becca Schwartz, Dean Barduka, Dirk Lehmann, Emily McArdle, Eric Moeller, Fraser Larock, Helen Sanderson, Helena Escalante, Ian Scott, Kaci Kai, Karishma Oza, Kristen Schnare, Kirsty Stark, Laura Lazar, Lisa Guida, Marie Schacht, MCK, Peter Shepherd, Robert Metcalf, Sam Meikle, Seth Godin, Taft Weber-Kilpack, Vince Mancari, Wisdom 2.0 attendees, and Yamini Oseguera-Bhatnagar.

Brent Lamphier, you have championed me and this work beyond. I feel lucky to be in your orbit.

Margit Pschick, you have been the best designer in my back pocket a girl could ever ask for. Also, thank you for saving me from the pigeon.

I may write another book just to be in conversation with Chantel Hamilton at Afterwords Communications, an editor with incomparable brilliance, insight, and vision. Being seen by you was profound. Thank you.

There is a bounty of love and life surrounding me. Transcendental writing teacher—Cary Tennis. Extraordinary fountain of money wisdom—Elizabeth Husserl. The Compassionate Witness of my personal journey—Matthew Morey. Extraordinary friends beyond measure—Heather Ladov, Jen Lucky, Vanessa Sabresse, Pippa Wiley, and Lisa Eddy.

Sandra Hesla is my family's everthere. Thanks for the food, the encouragement, and being my very own 411 and 911.

Taft, Sheldon, and Noah, one of my greatest joys is breathing the same air as you. Our life is magical and grand. You are my favorite adventure.

ABOUT THE AUTHOR

Shannon Weber believes you can thrive at the intersection of empathy and resilience.

By day, Shannon leads efforts to end HIV. By night, she hangs anonymous love notes in public spaces with her three teenagers. She is a serial social entrepreneur, having launched several HIV-informed sexual and reproductive health initiatives that have served thousands locally and impacted tens of thousands around the globe. Shannon has a Master's of Social Work from Tulane University, New Orleans, received the 2018 UCSF Chancellor's Award for Public Service, and has taught on stages from Durban to Hong Kong.

Learn more about empathy and resilience at
www.ShowUpHard.com.

Made in the USA
San Bernardino, CA
18 January 2019